PIANO • VOCAL • GUITAR

HIT TV & MOVIE SONGS

Disney and Disney/Pixar characters and artwork © Disney Enterprises, Inc

ISBN 978-1-4950-7416-5

7777 W. BLUEMOUND RD. P.O. BOX 13819 MILWAUKEE, WI 53213

Visit Hal Leonard Online at
www.halleonard.com

THE BOOK THIEF
from THE BOOK THIEF

Composed by
JOHN WILLIAMS

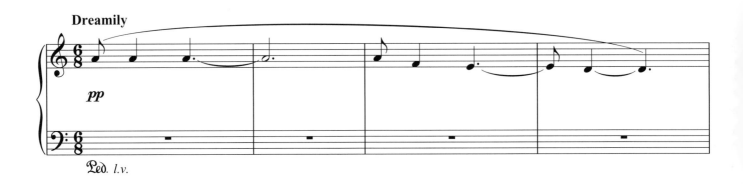

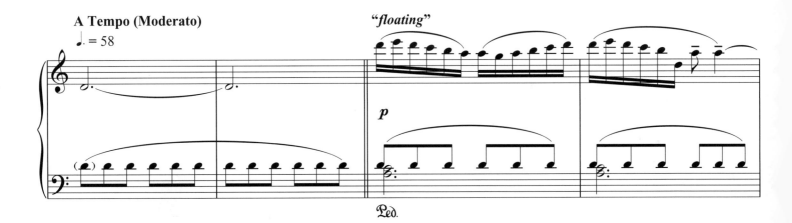

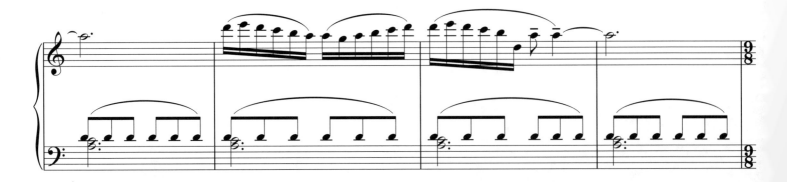

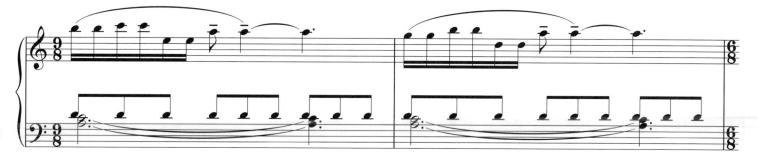

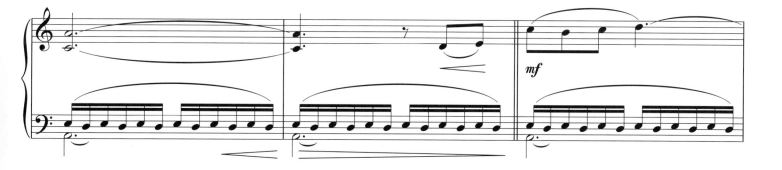

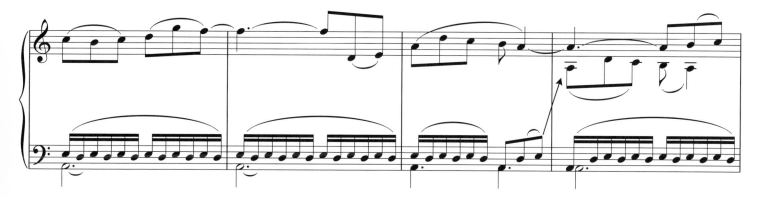

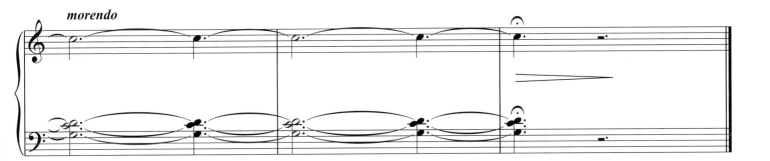

BOOM CLAP

from the Motion Picture Soundtrack THE FAULT IN OUR STARS

Words and Music by CHARLOTTE AITCHISON,
PATRIK BERGER, FREDRIK BERGER
and STEFAN GRASLUND

Moderate Pop Rock

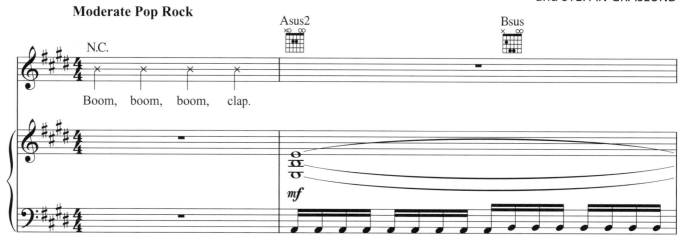

Boom, boom, boom, clap.

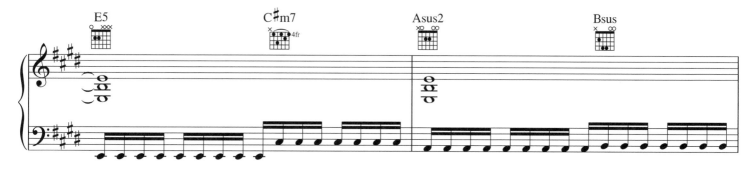

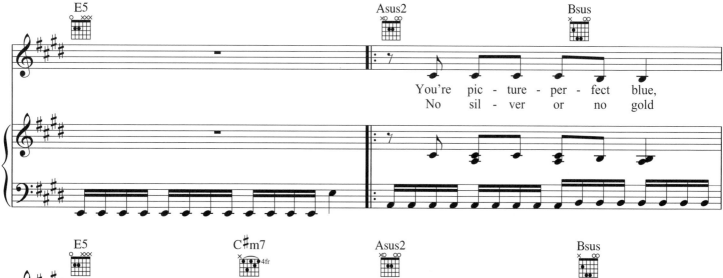

You're pic-ture-per-fect blue,
No sil-ver or no gold

sun-bath-ing on the moon.
could dress me up so good.

Stars shin-ing as your bones il-lu-mi-
You're the glit-ter in the dark-ness of my

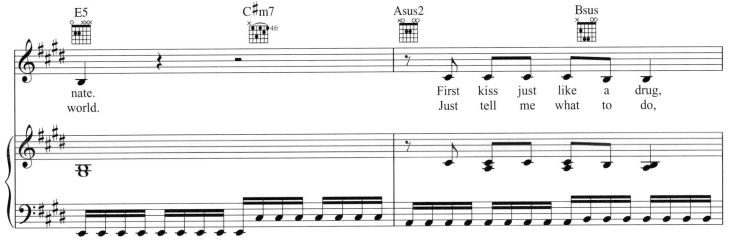

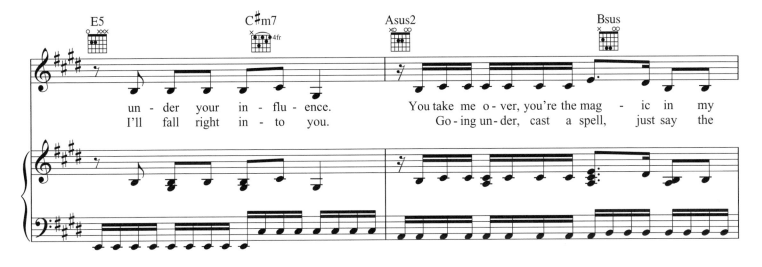

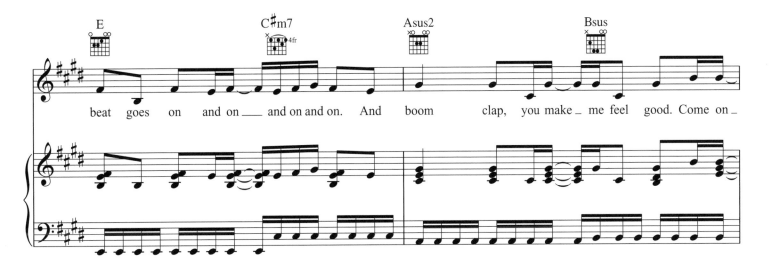

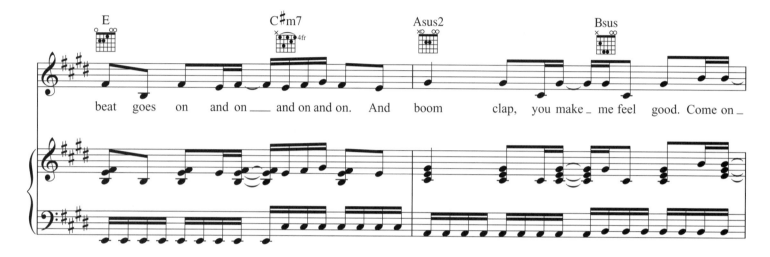

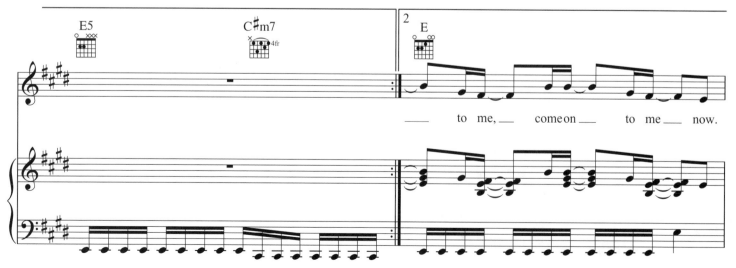

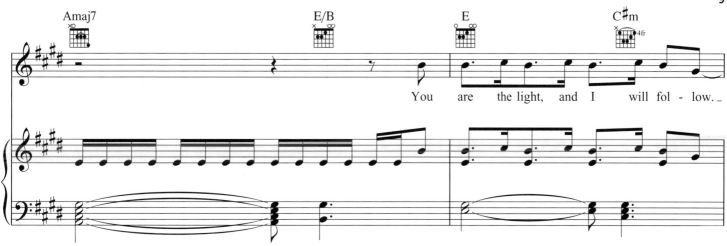

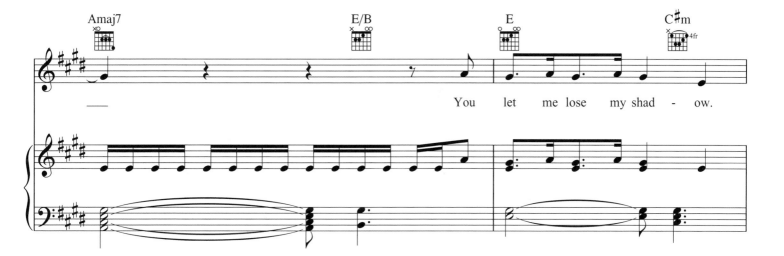

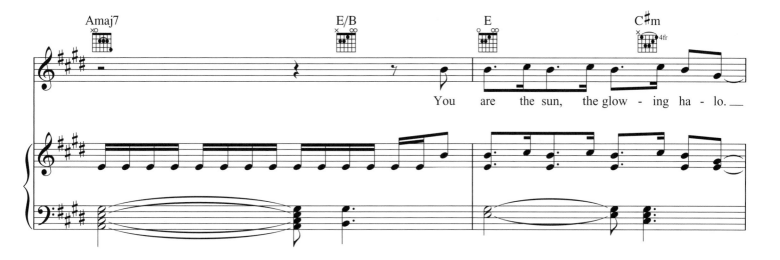

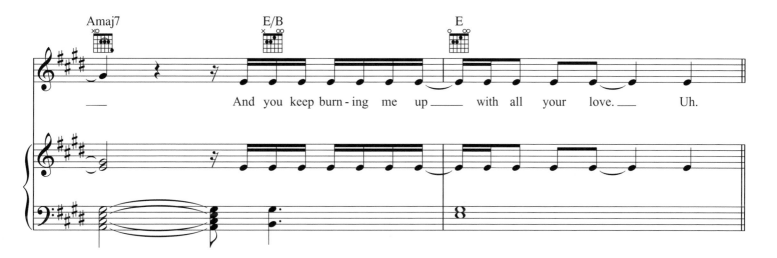

DEXTER MAIN TITLE

from the Television Series DEXTER

Words and Music by
ROLFE KENT

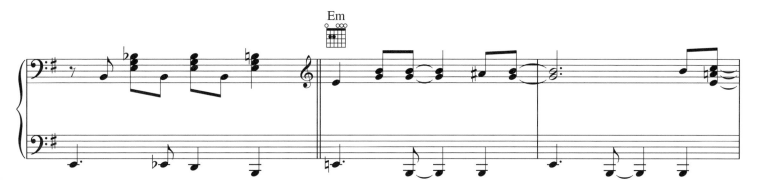

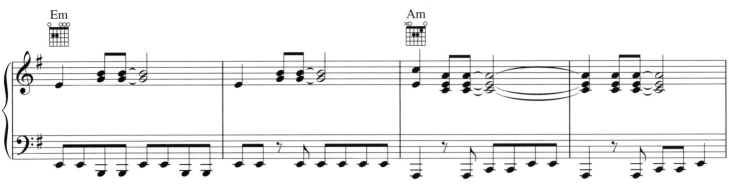

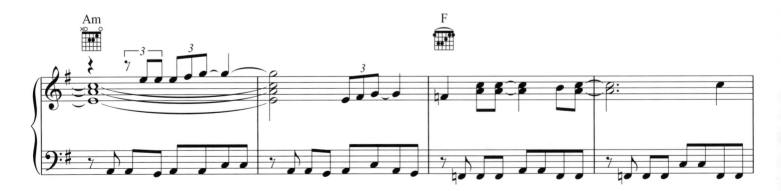

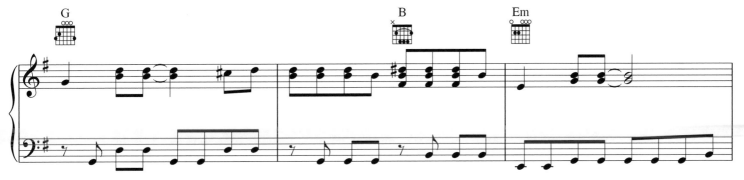

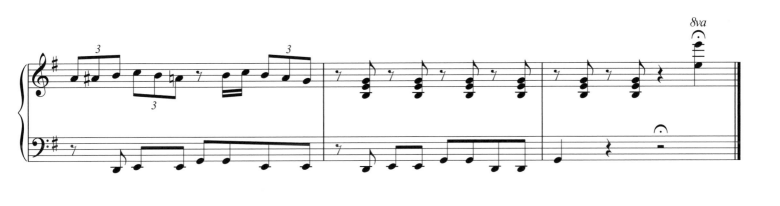

CAN'T STOP THE FEELING
from TROLLS

Words and Music by JUSTIN TIMBERLAKE,
MAX MARTIN and SHELLBACK

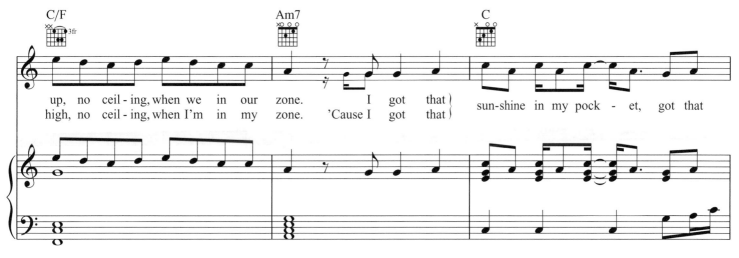
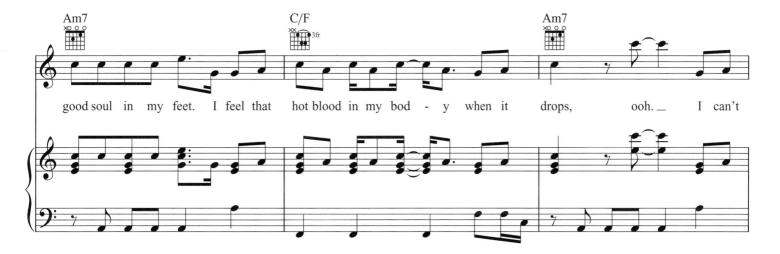
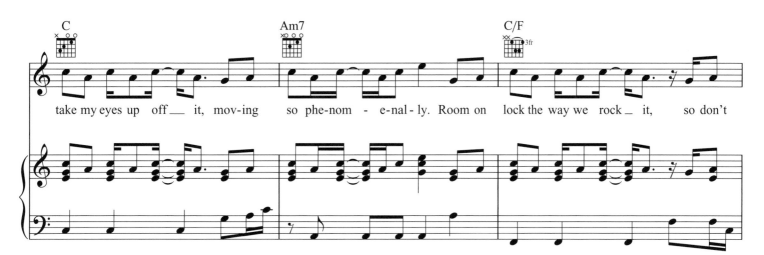
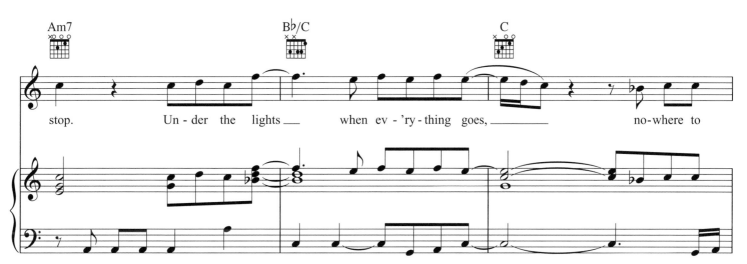

hide when I'm get-ting you close. _____ When we move, _____ well, you al - read - y know. __

_____ So just i - mag - ine, _____

(just i - mag - ine,) _____

(just i - mag - ine.) _____

Noth-ing I __ can see __ but you __ when you dance, dance, dance. I feel a good, __

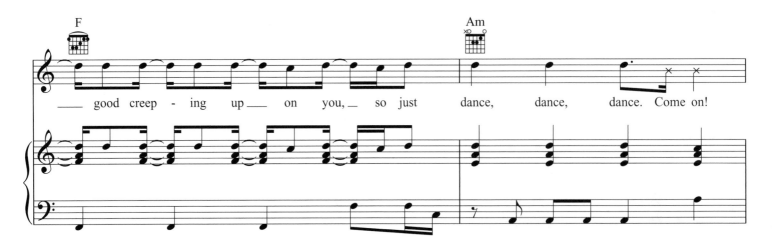

__ good creep - ing up __ on you, __ so just dance, dance, dance. Come on!

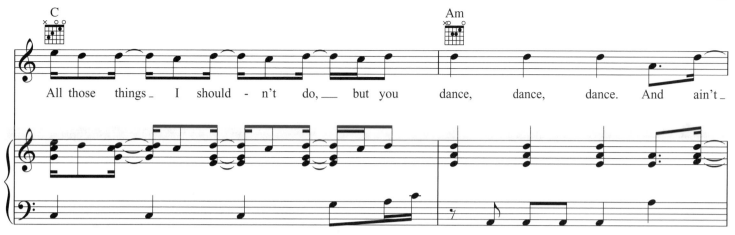

I can't stop the feel - ing. _____ Got this feel - ing in my
bod - y. _____

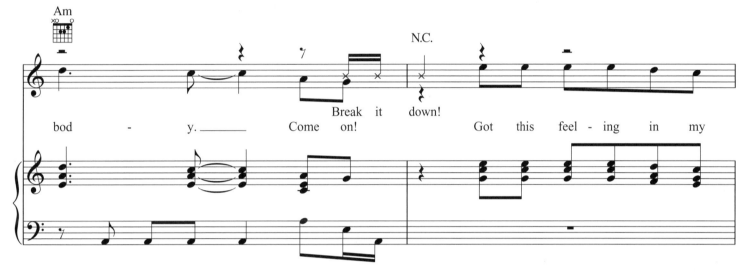

bod - y. _____ Come on! Break it down! Got this feel - ing in my

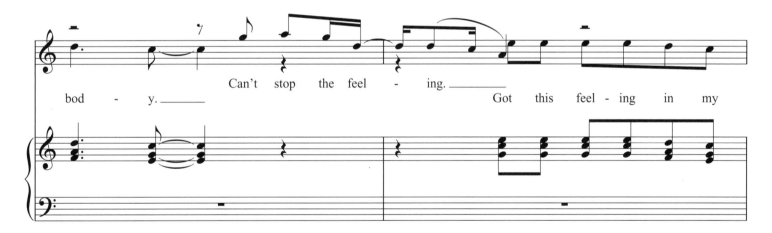

bod - y. _____ Can't stop the feel - ing. _____ Got this feel - ing in my

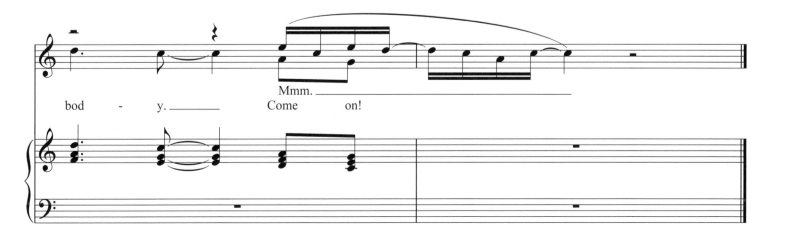

bod - y. _____ Come on!
Mmm. _____

COME JOIN THE MURDER

from SONS OF ANARCHY

Words and Music by BOB THIELE,
KURT SUTTER and JACOB SMITH

You'll __ touch the hand __ of God, __ and He'll __ make you king,

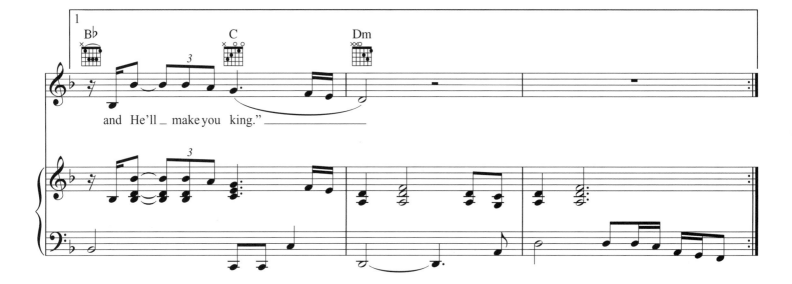

and He'll __ make you king." ____

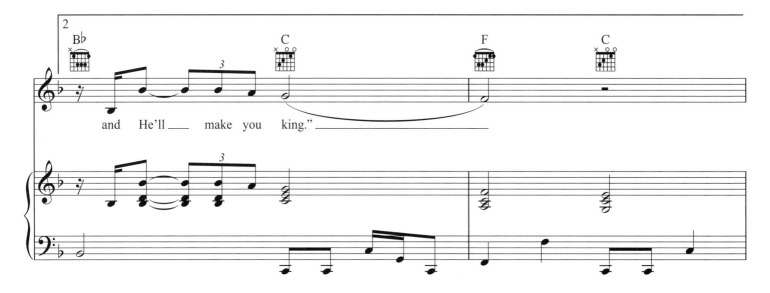

and He'll ____ make you king." ____

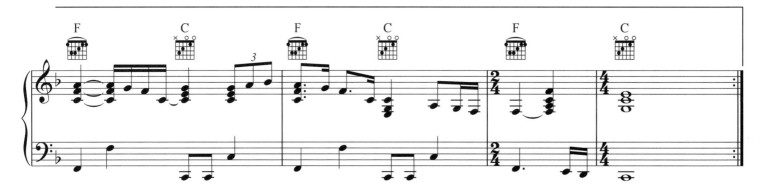

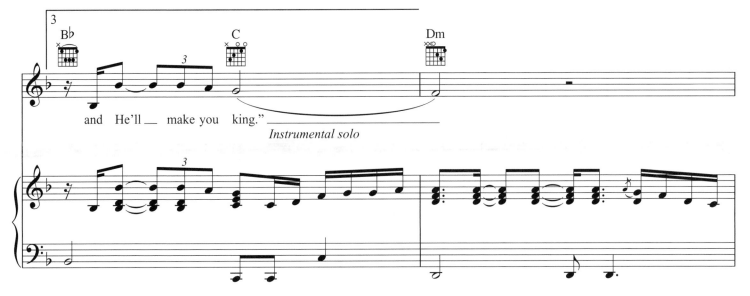

and He'll __ make you king." _____
Instrumental solo

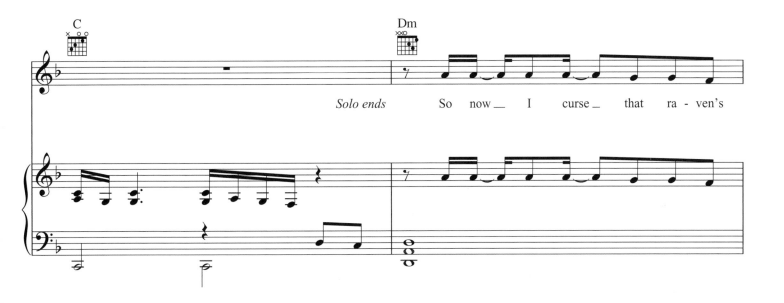

Solo ends So now __ I curse __ that ra - ven's

fi - re: "You made me hate, ___ you made me burn." He

laughed a - loud ___ as ___ he flew ___ from E - den, "You al - ways

knew. You nev - er learn." The crow no long - er sings to me, like ___

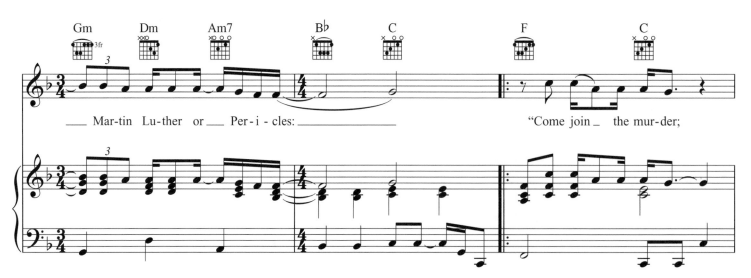

___ Mar - tin Lu - ther or ___ Per - i - cles: _____ "Come join ___ the mur - der;

CONQUEROR

from EMPIRE

Words and Music by AKIL KING, KYLE OWENS,
JOHN LARDIERI, JARAMYE DANIELS, CLAUDE KELLY,
ESTELLE SWARAY, SHARIF SLATER and ANGEL HIGGS

Well, we all ___ make mis- takes. ___ You might fall ___ on your face, _____ but you got- ta get

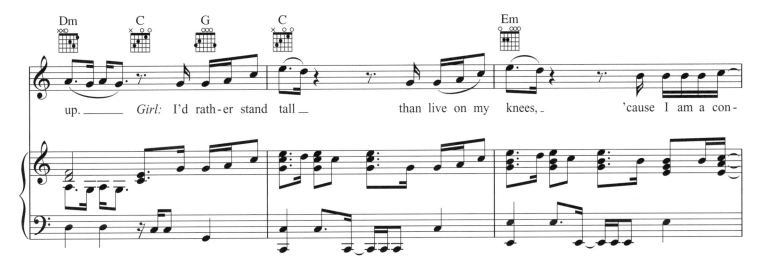

up. _____ *Girl:* I'd rath- er stand tall ___ than live on my knees, _ 'cause I am a con-

- quer- or, _____ and I won't ac- cept ___ de- feat. _____ Try tell- in' me

no. _____ One thing a- bout me _____ is I am a con-

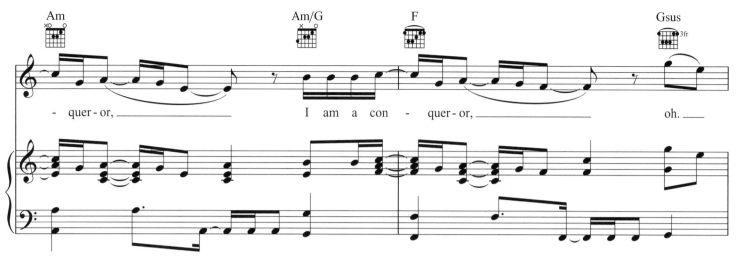

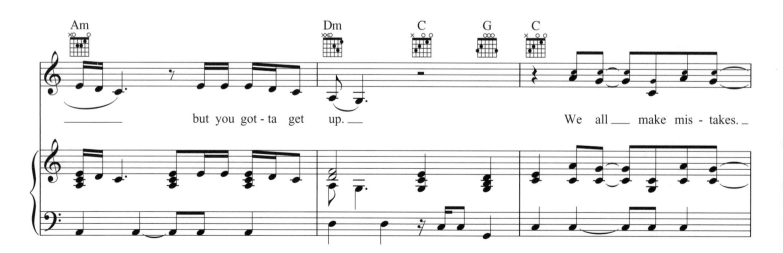

D.S. al Coda

You might fall____ on your face._____ Don't ev - er give up._____ I'd rath - er stand

We all_____ make mis - takes.____ You might fall_____ on your face,_____

_____ but I am a con - quer - or._____

DOWNTON ABBEY
(Theme)

Music by
JOHN LUNN

Con moto ♩ = 167

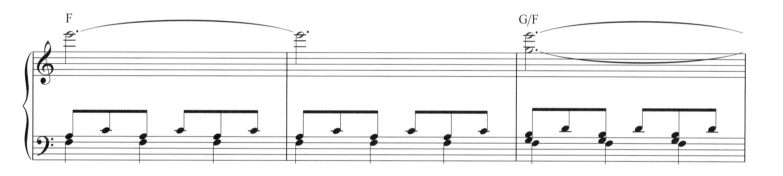

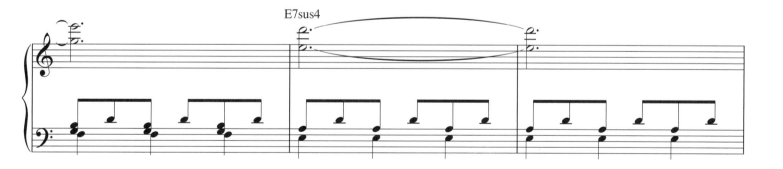

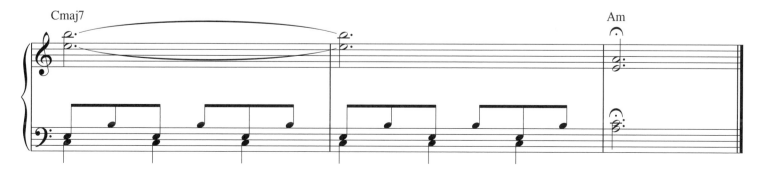

EVEN MORE MINE

from MY BIG FAT GREEK WEDDING 2

Words and Music by NATHAN CHAPMAN,
RITA WILSON and DARRELL BROWN

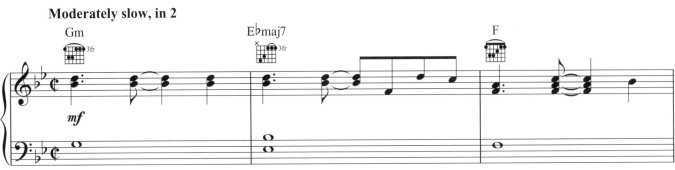

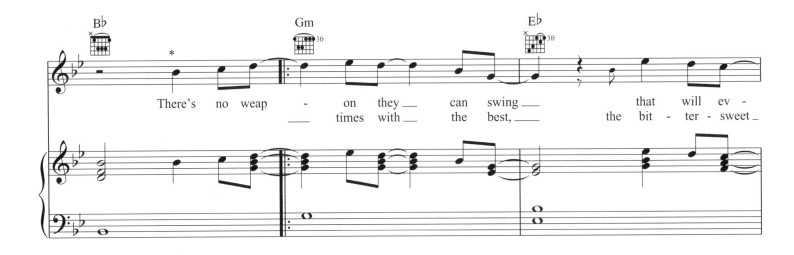

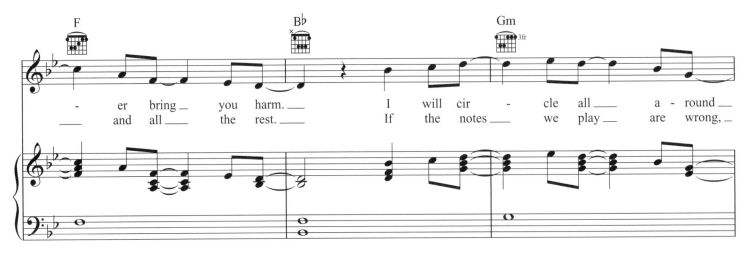

* Vocal sung an octave lower than written.

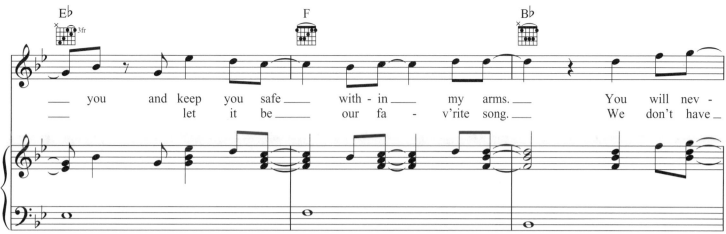

you and keep you safe___ with - in___ my arms.___ You will nev -
let it be___ our fa - v'rite song.___ We don't have___

- er feel___ a - ban - doned; I will push___ the world___ a - side.___
to win___ it all,___ we don't need___ it all___ to rhyme.___

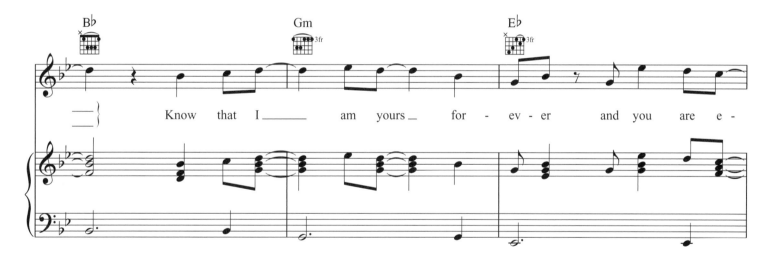

Know that I___ am yours___ for - ev - er and you are e -

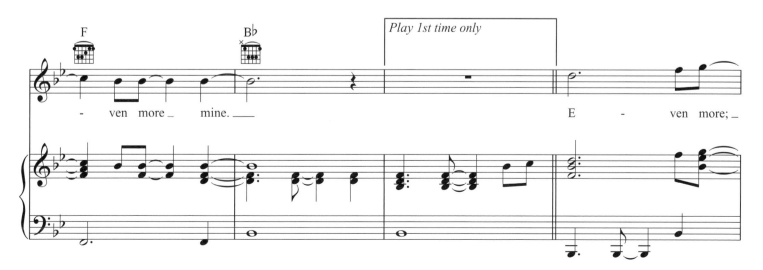

Play 1st time only

- ven more___ mine.___   E - ven more;___

for all the ways_ I'm yours,_ you_ are e - ven more_

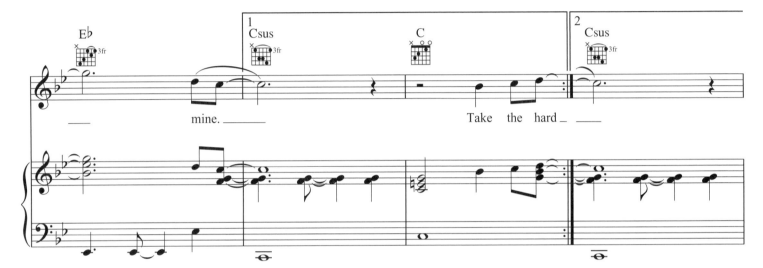

_ mine._ Take the hard_ _

E - ven more;_ for all the ways_ I'm yours,_

_ you_ are e - ven more;_ mine._

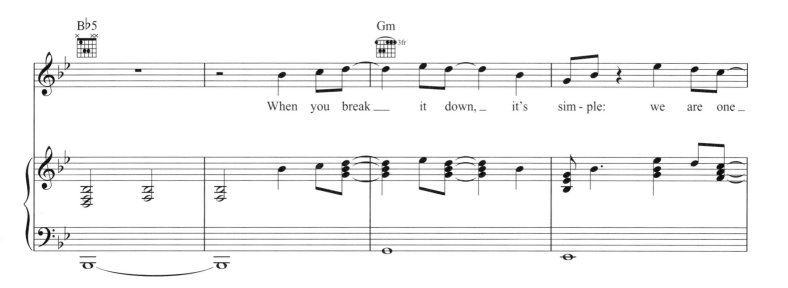

When you break ___ it down, ___ it's sim - ple: we are one ___

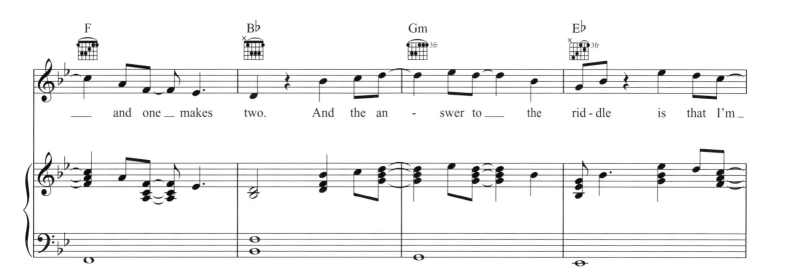

___ and one ___ makes two. And the an - swer to ___ the rid - dle is that I'm ___

___ in love ___ with you. ___ Oh, the fu - ture we ___ have wait - ing, a

great - er hand ___ de - signed, ___ so that I _____ am yours for -

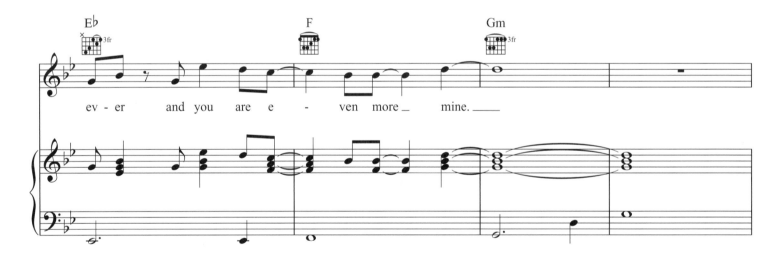

ev - er and you are e - ven more ___ mine. _____

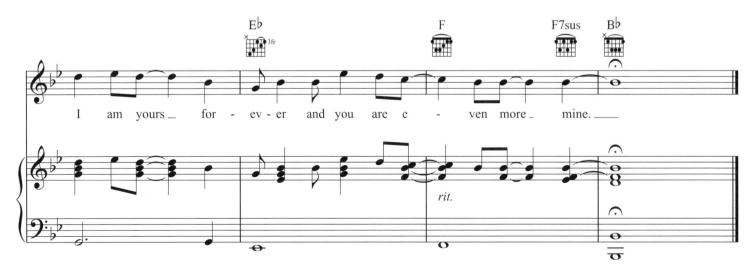

I am yours ___ for - ev - er and you are e - ven more ___ mine. _____

rit.

FINDING DORY
(Main Title)
from the Walt Disney/Pixar film FINDING DORY

Music by
THOMAS NEWMAN

Moderately

Pedal ad lib. throughout

FLASHLIGHT
from PITCH PERFECT 2

Words and Music by SIA FURLER,
CHRISTIAN GUZMAN, SAM SMITH,
JASON MOORE and MARIO MEJIA

Moderate Ballad

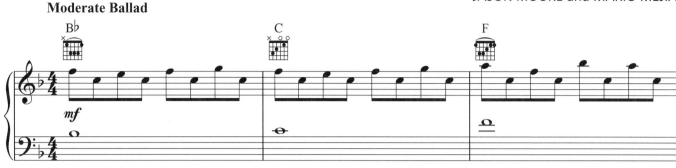

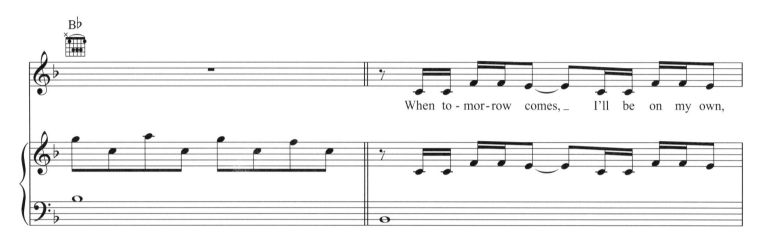

When to-mor-row comes, _ I'll be on my own, feel-ing fright-ened of ___ the things that I don't know. _ When to-mor-row _ comes, _ to-mor-row _ comes,

___ to-mor-row ___ comes.

And though the road is long, _ I look up to the sky.
I see the shad - ows long be-neath the moun-tain top.

(cued note on repeat)

And in the dark I found__ lost hope that I won't fly,   and I sing a-lone,   I sing a-lone,
I'm not a-fraid__ when the rain won't stop,   'cause you light the way,   you light the way,

then I sing a-lone._____   I got all I need when I got you and I.__
you light the way._____

I look a-round me and see sweet life.   I'm stuck in the dark, but you're my flash-light.

You're get-ting me, get-ting me through the night.___   Can't stop my heart when you're shin-ing in my

44

46

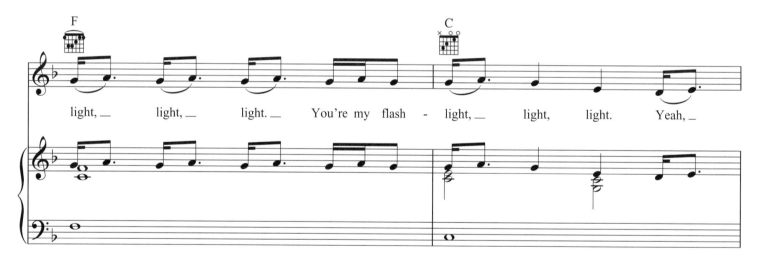

HERE COMES THE LION GUARD

from the Disney Channel Series THE LION GUARD

Words and Music by BEAU BLACK,
SARAH MIRZA and FORD RILEY

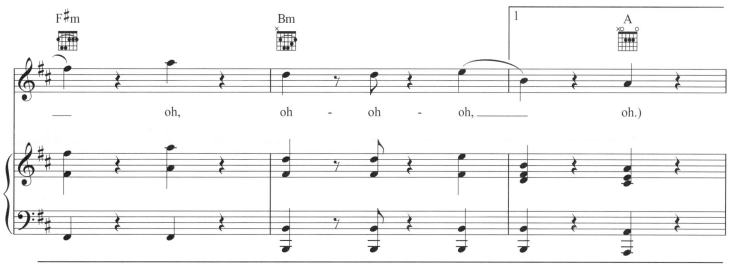

oh,   oh - oh - oh, _____   oh.)

So an - y time that trou - ble comes, _ there's a new ___ team

wait - ing   to take a stand, to   fight and keep the

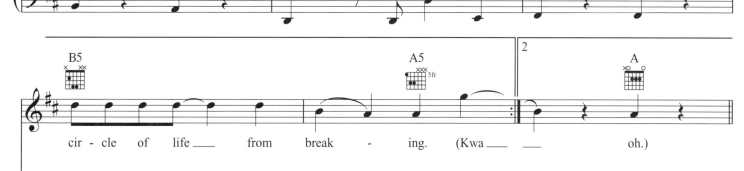

cir - cle of life ___ from break - ing. (Kwa ___ ___ oh.)

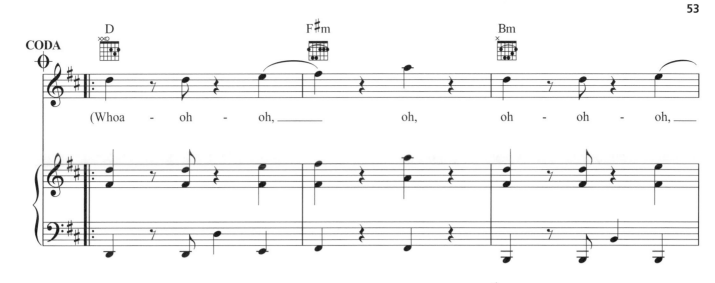

(Whoa - oh - oh, _____ oh, oh - oh - oh, _____

_____ oh.) (Whoa - oh - oh, _____ oh.)

Look out, here _____ comes the Li - on Guard.

Look out, here _____ comes the Li - on Guard.

HEATHENS

from SUICIDE SQUAD

Words and Music by
TYLER JOSEPH

Moderate groove

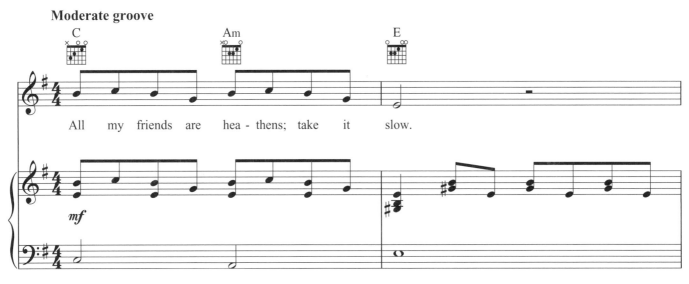

All my friends are hea - thens; take it slow.

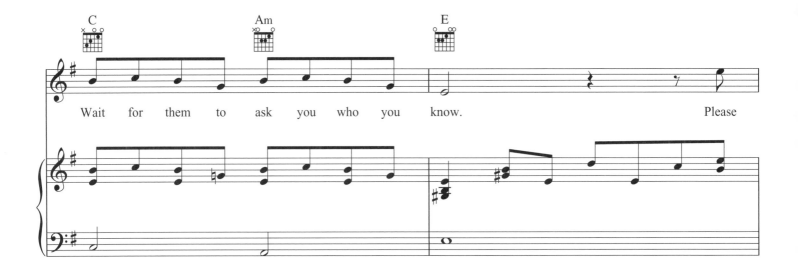

Wait for them to ask you who you know. Please

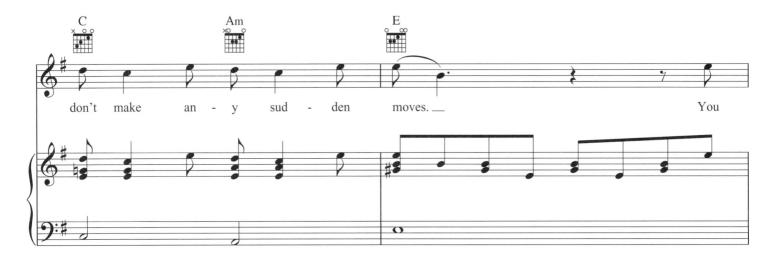

don't make an - y sud - den moves. _____ You

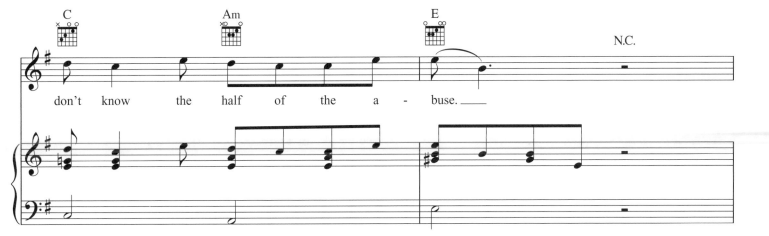

don't know the half of the a - buse. _____

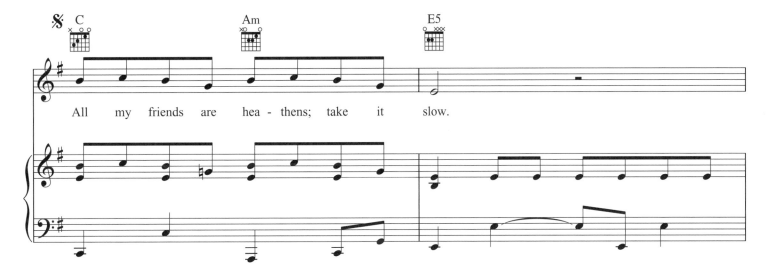

All my friends are hea - thens; take it slow.

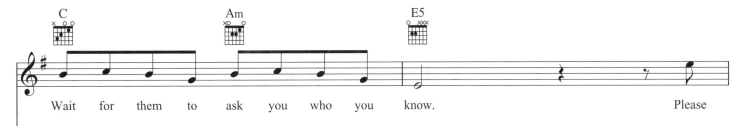

Wait for them to ask you who you know. Please

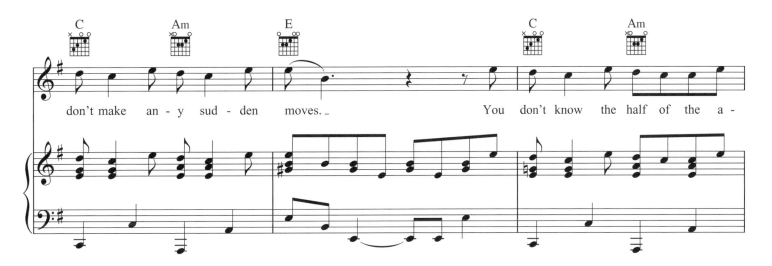

don't make an - y sud - den moves. _ You don't know the half of the a -

B
D.S. al Coda
you?" But af - ter all I've said, please don't for - get.
CODA
C
E5
We don't deal with out - sid - ers ver - y well. They say new - com - ers have a cer - tain smell.
Am
E5
You have trust is - sues, not to men - tion, they say they can smell your in - ten - tions.
C
Am
E5
You'll nev - er know the freak show sit - ting next to you. You'll have some weird peo - ple sit - ting next to

you. You'll think, "How did I get here, sit-ting next to you?" But af-ter all I've said,

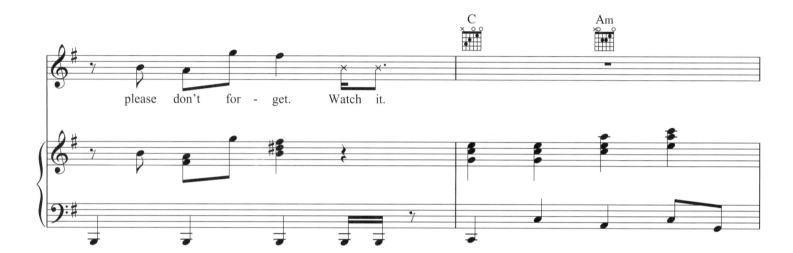

please don't for-get. Watch it.

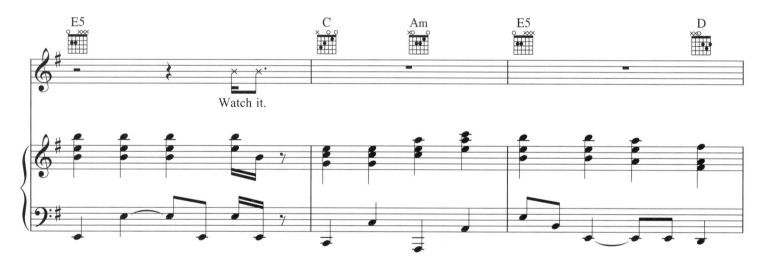

Watch it.

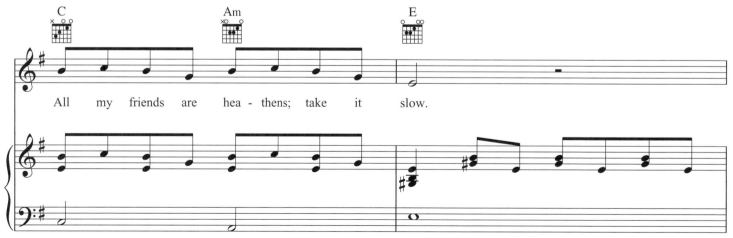

All my friends are hea-thens; take it slow.

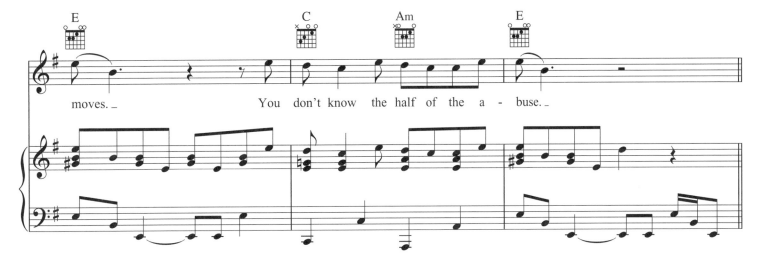

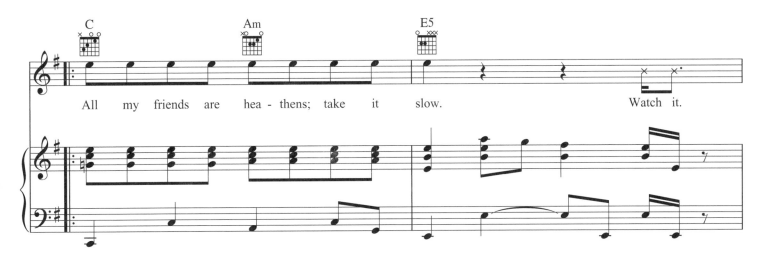

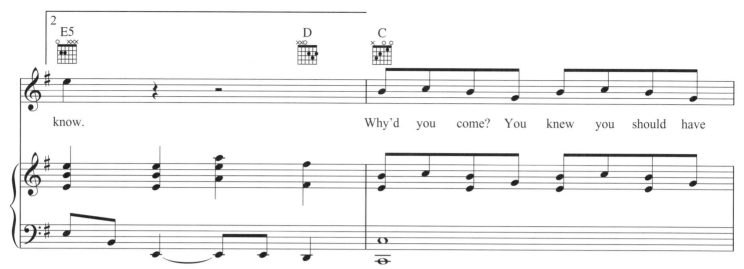

know.   Why'd you come? You knew you should have

stayed.   I tried to warn you just to stay a —

way.   And now they're out - side, read - y to

bust.   It looks like you might be one of us.

HOMESTEAD

from the Walt Disney/Pixar film THE GOOD DINOSAUR

Music and Lyrics by MYCHAEL DANNA
and JEFF DANNA

Moderately

Pedal ad lib. throughout

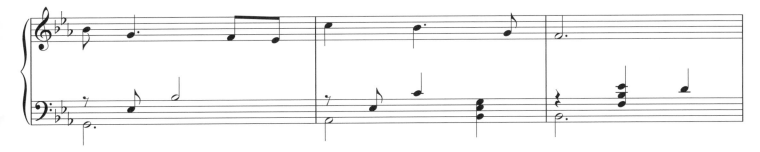

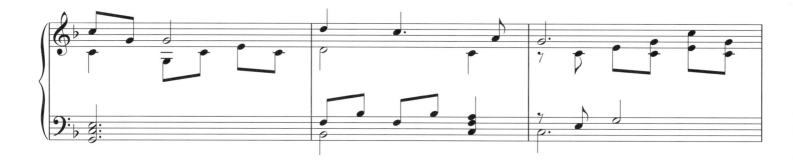

I LOVE YOU TOO MUCH

from THE BOOK OF LIFE

Lyric by PAUL WILLIAMS
Music by GUSTAVO SANTAOLALLA

Moderately slow

With pedal

I love _____ you too much _____ to
live _____ for your touch;

live with - out you lov - ing me back. I love _____ you too
whis - per your name night af - ter night. I love _____ you too

much; Heav - en's my wit - ness, and this is a fact.) I
much; there's on - ly one feel - ing, and I know it's right.)

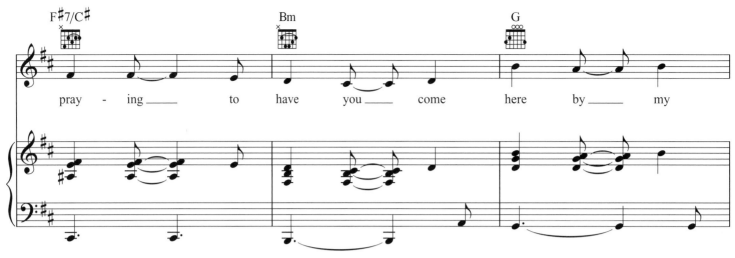

pray - ing _____ to have you _____ come here by _____ my

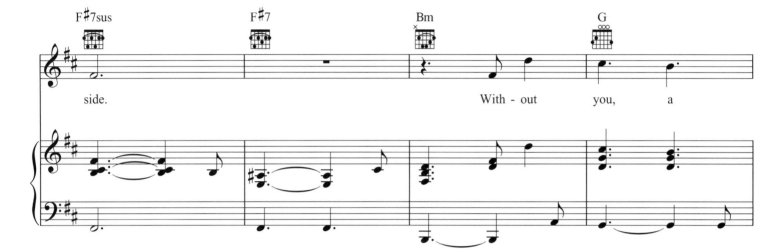

side. With - out you, a

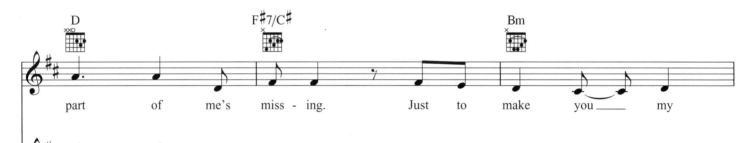

part of me's miss - ing. Just to make you _____ my

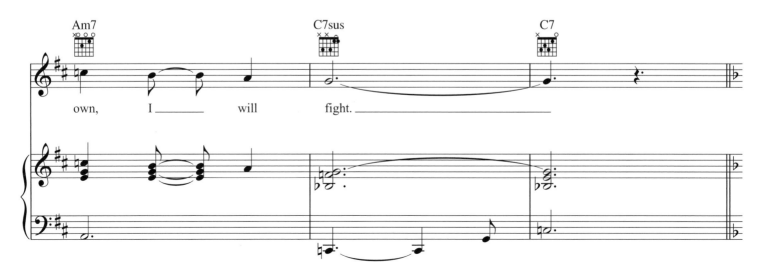

own, I _____ will fight. _____

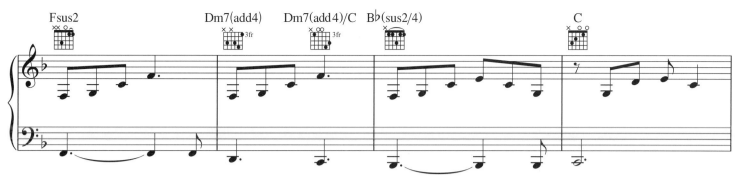

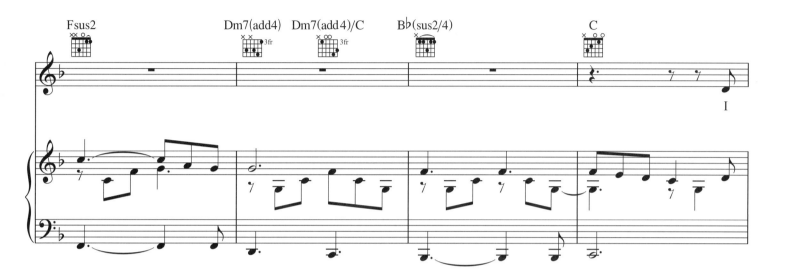

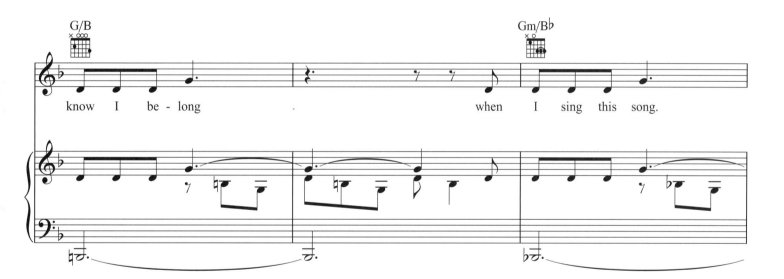

know I be-long when I sing this song.

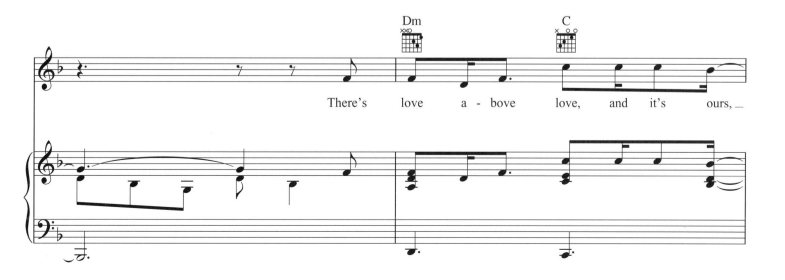

There's love a-bove love, and it's ours, __

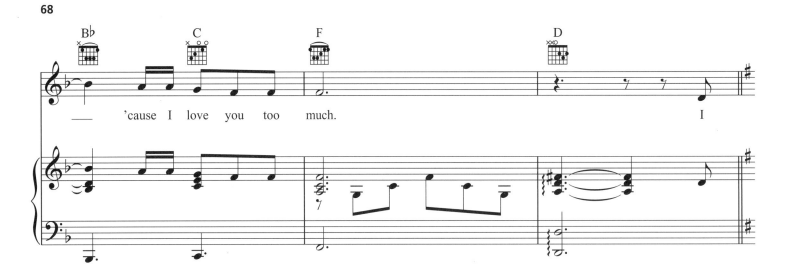

'cause I love you too much. I

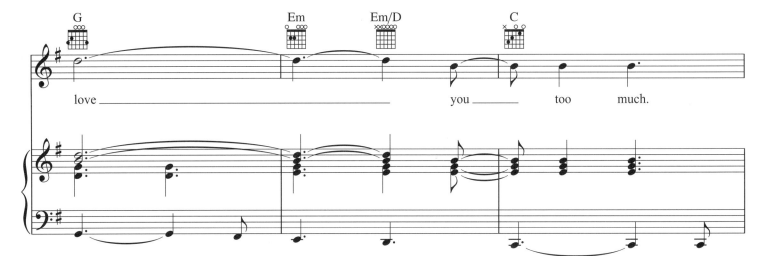

love _____ you ___ too much.

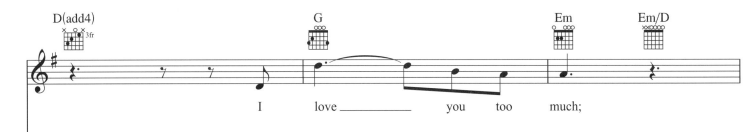

I love _____ you too much;

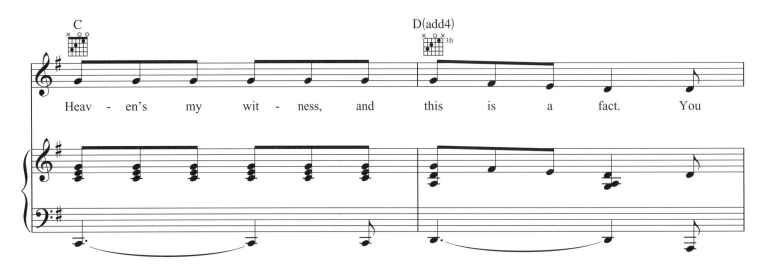

Heav-en's my wit-ness, and this is a fact. You

live in my soul. _____ Your heart is my goal. _____

_____ There's love a - bove love, and it's mine, 'cause I love you. There's

love a - bove love, and it's yours, 'cause I love you. There's

love a - bove love, and it's ours if you love me as much.

LAVA
from LAVA

Music and Lyrics by
JAMES FORD MURPHY

Easy half-time feel

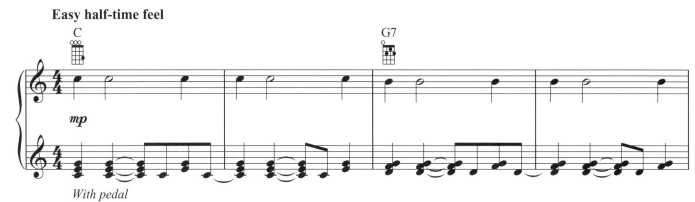

mp

With pedal

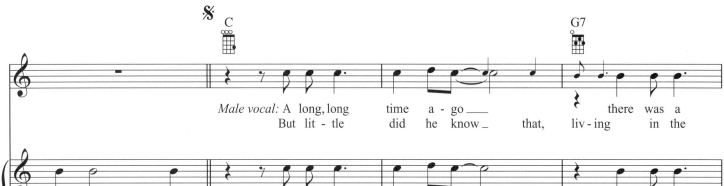

Male vocal: A long, long time a - go ____ there was a
But lit - tle did he know ____ that, liv - ing in the

2nd time: a tempo

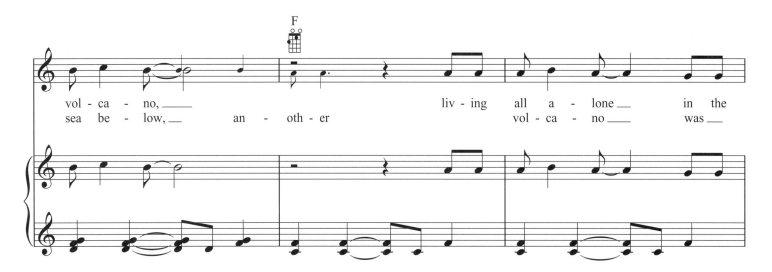

vol - ca - no, _____ living all a - lone ____ in the
sea be - low, ____ an - oth - er vol - ca - no ____ was ____

mid - dle of ___ the sea.
lis - ten - ing to his song.
He sat high a -
Ev - 'ry day she

bove his bay, ___
heard his tune, ___
watch - ing all the cou - ples play, ___
her ___ la - va grew and grew, ___ be -

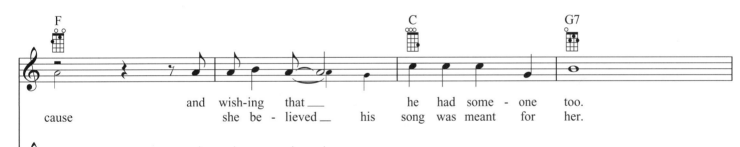

cause
and wish - ing that ___
she be - lieved ___ his
he had some - one too.
song was meant for her.

And from his la - va came ___ this song of hope
Now she was so read - y ___ to meet ___ him a -

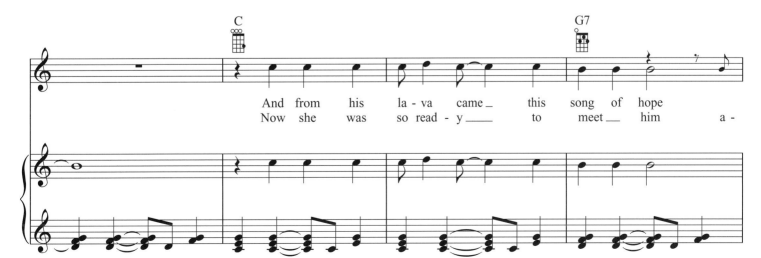

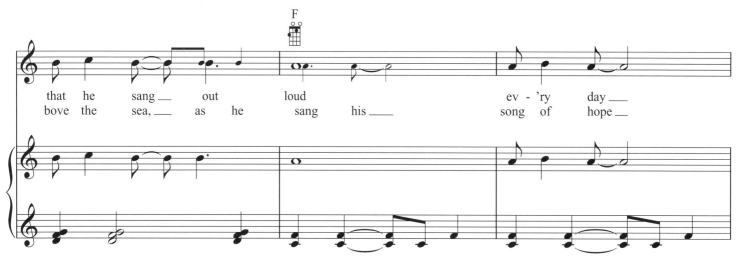

that he sang ___ out loud ev - 'ry day ___
bove the sea, ___ as he sang his ___ song of hope ___

for years ___ and years. }
for the ___ last time. }

2nd time: Slower

"I have a dream ___

___ I hope will ___ come true, that you're here ___ with

me, and I'm here ___ with you. I wish that ___ the

earth, sea,_ and the sky up _ a - bove - a will send me

some - one to la - va." _

Years of sing-ing all a - lone _ turned his la - va

into stone,___ un - til he was on ___ the brink of ex - tinc -

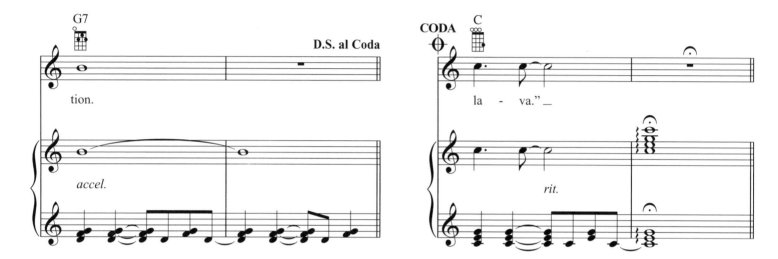

tion.   *accel.*   **D.S. al Coda**

CODA   la - va."___   *rit.*

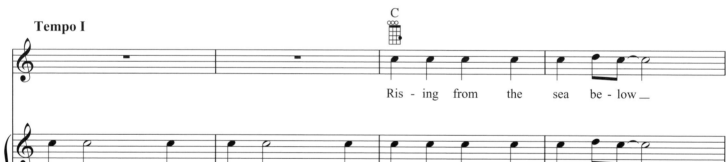

Tempo I

Ris - ing from the sea be - low ___

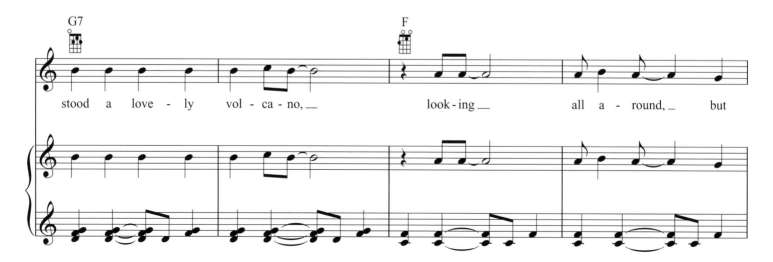

stood a love - ly vol - ca - no, ___ look - ing ___ all a - round, ___ but

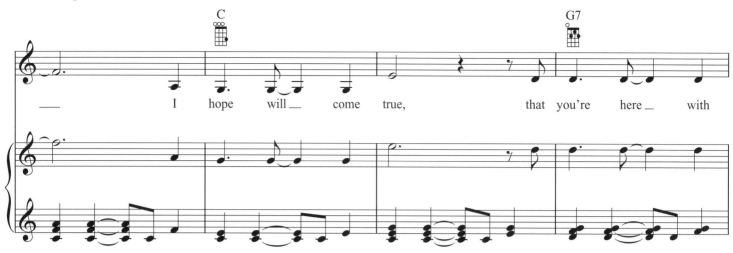

I hope will __ come true, that you're here __ with

me, and I'm here __ with you. I _____ wish that __ the

earth, sea, __ and the sky up __ a - bove - a will send me

some-one to la - va." _____

I'll grow old with you. ___
(Ah.) ___ We thank ___ the earth, sea, ___ and the

sky we ___ thank ___ too, I la-va

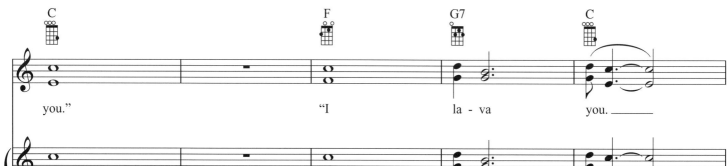

you." "I la-va you. ___

I la-va you." ___

JUST LIKE FIRE

from ALICE THROUGH THE LOOKING GLASS (WDP)

Words and Music by ALECIA MOORE,
MAX MARTIN, SHELLBACK
and OSCAR HOLTER

Vocal sung an octave lower than written.

walk-in' on a wire,____ try-in' to go high-er. Feels like I'm sur-round-ed by clowns____ and li-ars.
no mat-ter the weath-er, we can do it bet-ter, you and me to-geth-er, for-ev - er and ev-er.

E - ven when I give it all a-way, I want it all,_____ mm._____ (We came here to
We don't have to wor-ry 'bout a thing, a-bout a thing,____ no._____

run it, run it, run it. We came here to run it, run it,

run it.) Just like fi-re, burn-ing up the way, if I can light the

** *Vocal sung at written pitch.*

Additional Lyrics

Rap: So look, I came here to run it, just 'cause nobody's done it.
Y'all don't think I could run it, but look, I've been here, I've done it.
Impossible? Please! Watch, I do it with ease.
You just gotta believe. Come on, come on with me.

THE LIGHT
featured in SCANDAL

By JAMES LaVALLE
and MATTHEW RESOVICH

Moderately slow

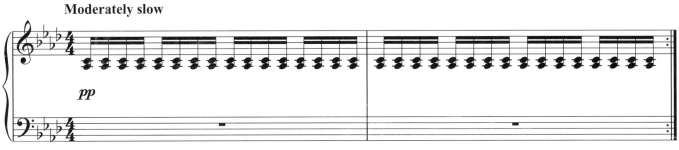

pp

Pedal ad lib. throughout

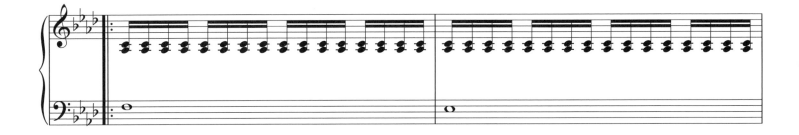

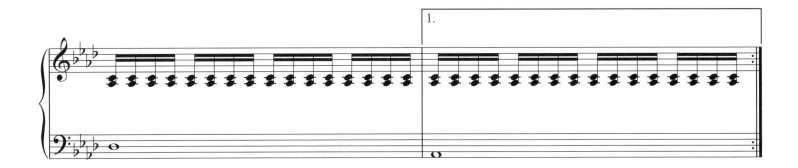

1.

2.

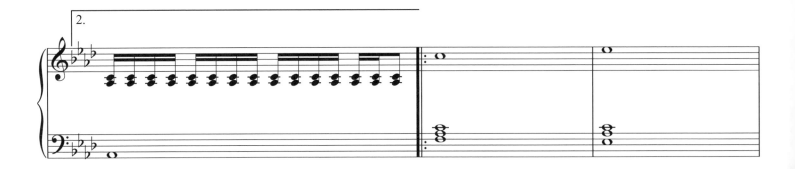

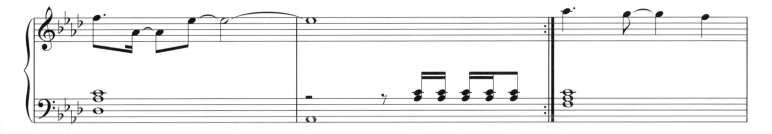

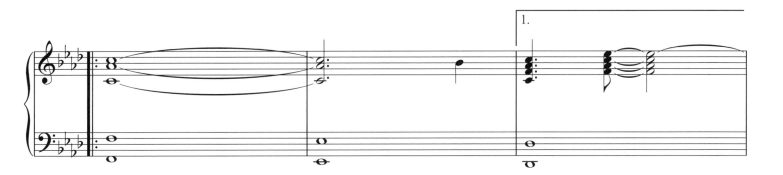

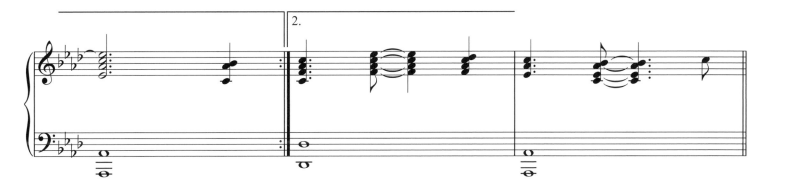

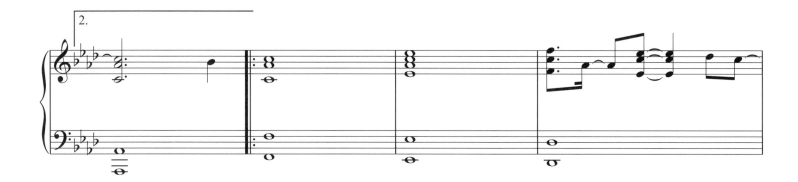

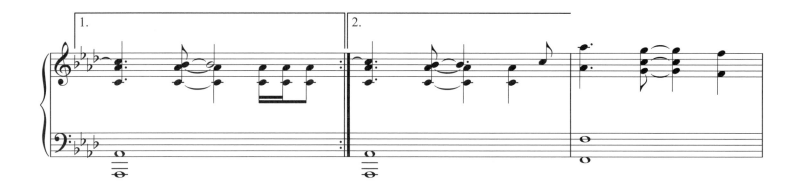

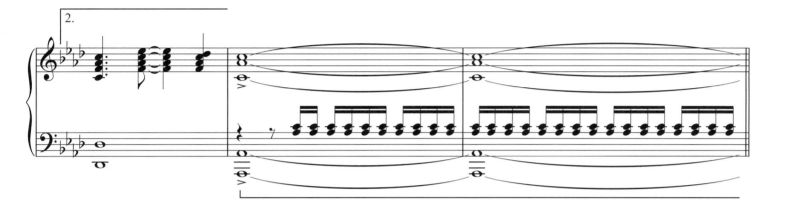

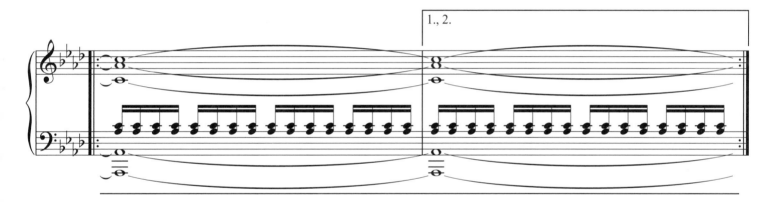

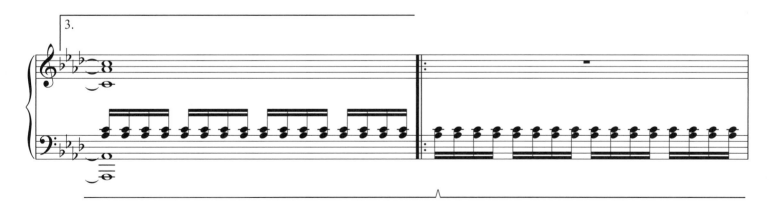

Repeat and Fade   **Optional Ending**

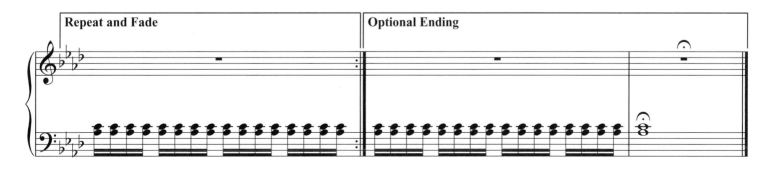

LIGHT OF THE SEVEN
from the HBO Series GAME OF THRONES

By RAMIN DJAWADI

Rubato

mp

With pedal

rit.

a tempo

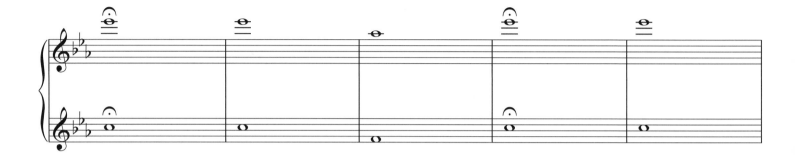

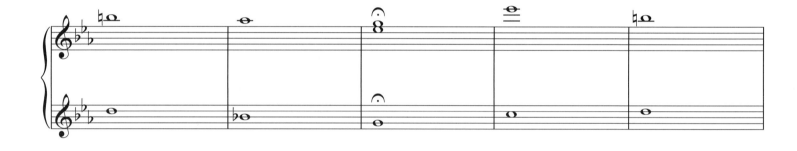

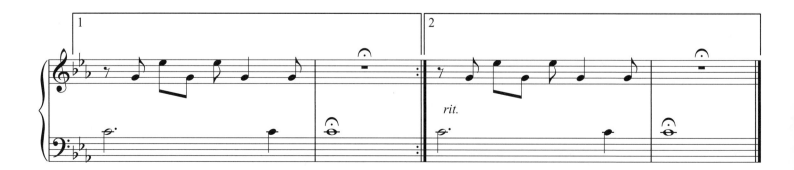

LOVE ME LIKE YOU DO
from FIFTY SHADES OF GREY

Words and Music by MAX MARTIN,
SAVAN KOTECHA, ILYA,
ALI PAYAMI and TOVE LO

Moderately slow

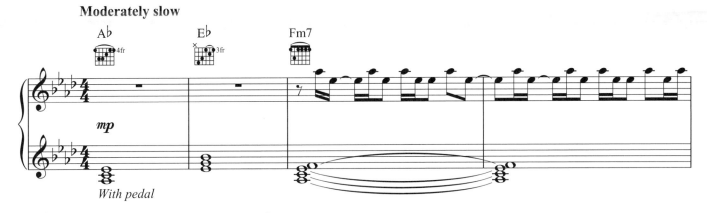

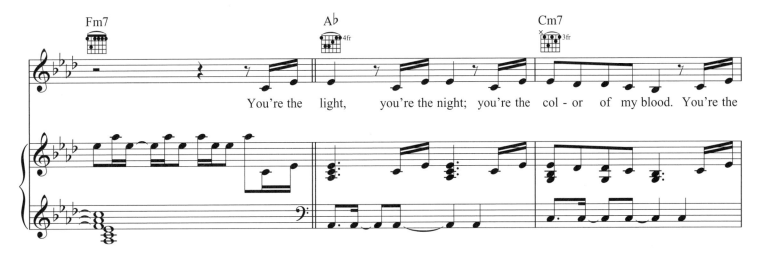

You're the light, you're the night; you're the col-or of my blood. You're the

cure, you're the pain; you're the on-ly thing I wan-na touch. _____ Nev-er

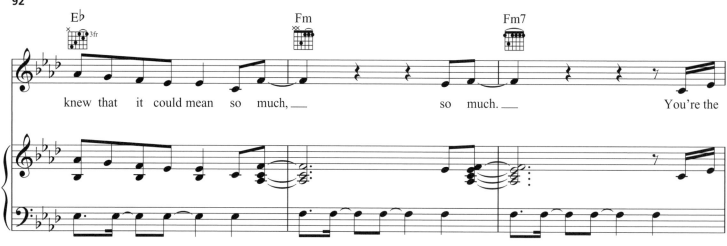

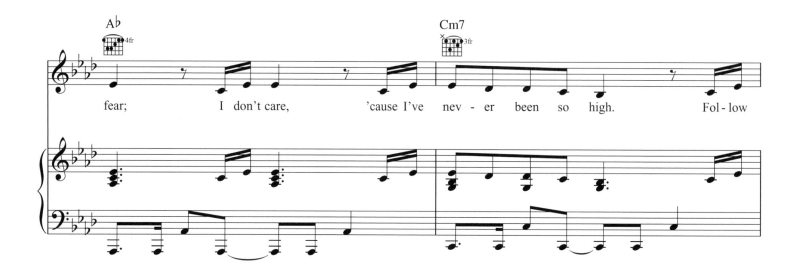

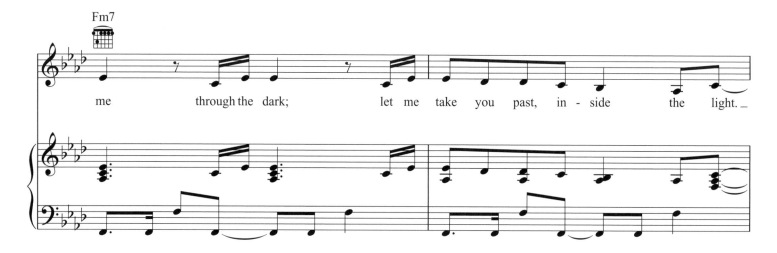

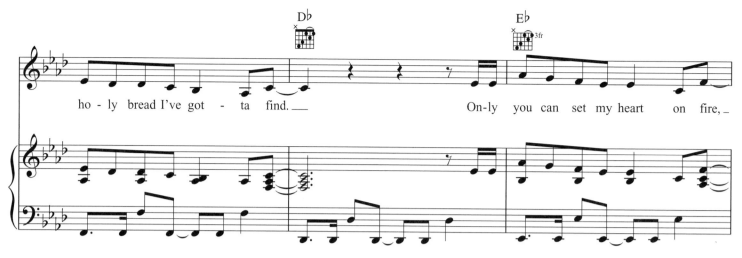

ho - ly bread I've got - ta find. __ On - ly you can set my heart on fire, _

__ on fire. __ Yeah, I'll let you __ set __ the pace, _

_____ 'cause I'm not __ think - ing straight. _____ My

head's spin - ning __ a - round, I ____ can't __ see clear no __ more. _

What are you wait - ing for? _____

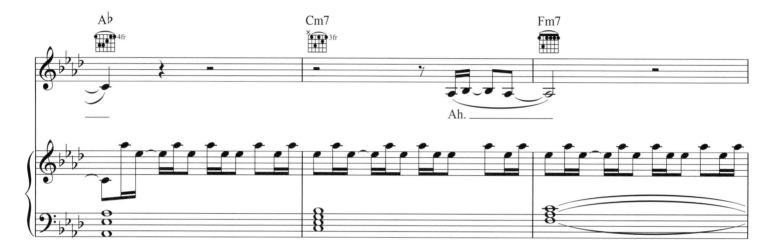

____ Ah. _____

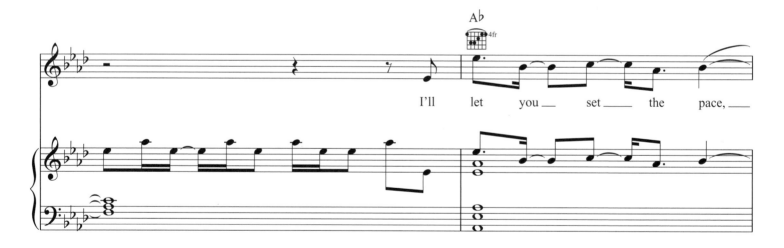

I'll let you __ set __ the pace, ____

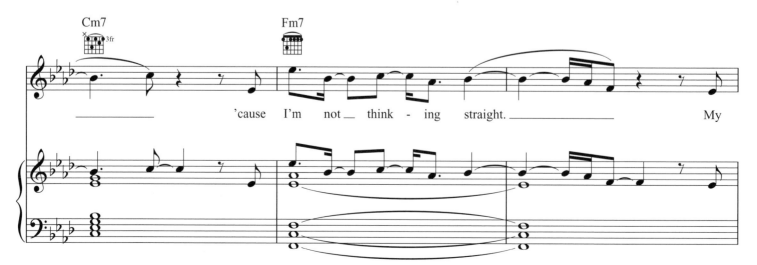

_____ 'cause I'm not __ think - ing straight. _____ My

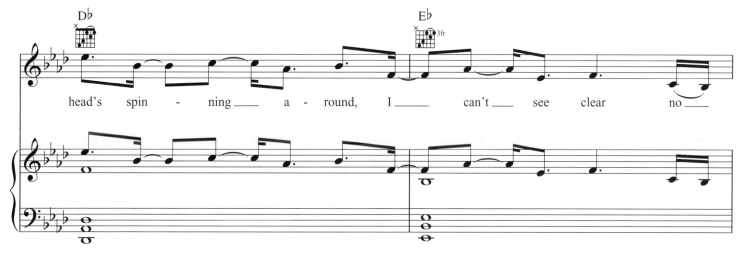

head's spin - ning __ a - round, I __ can't __ see clear no __

more. What are you wait - ing for? __

D.S. al Coda
(take repeat)

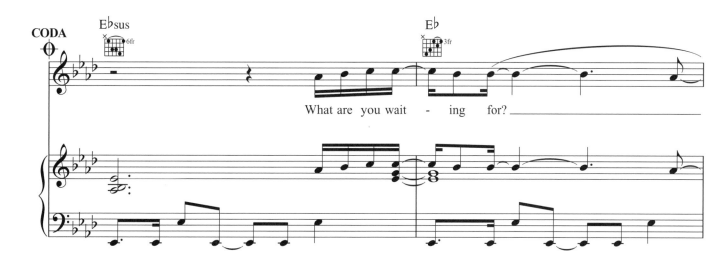

CODA

What are you wait - ing for? _____

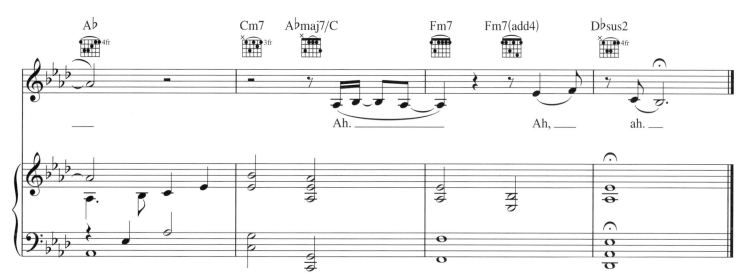

__ Ah. _____ Ah, __ ah. __

MARCH OF THE RESISTANCE
from STAR WARS: THE FORCE AWAKENS

Music by
JOHN WILLIAMS

Crisply

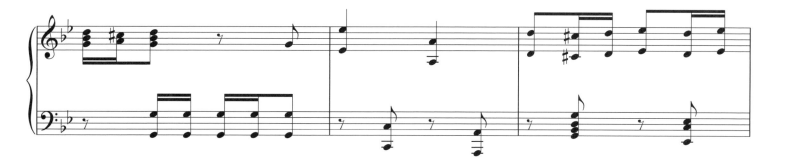

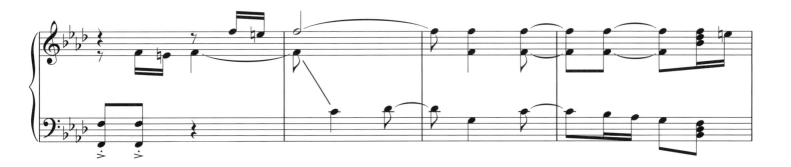

NEW AVENGERS–
AVENGERS: AGE OF ULTRON

from the Motion Picture AVENGERS: AGE OF ULTRON

Music by
DANNY ELFMAN

Slowly, expressively

Moderately, in 2, steadily

Moderately fast

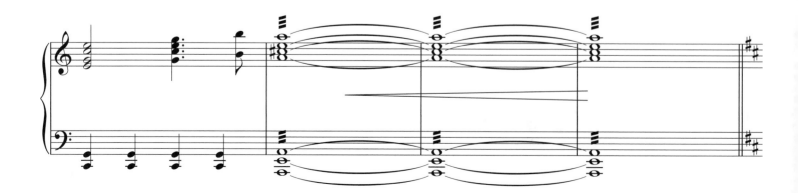

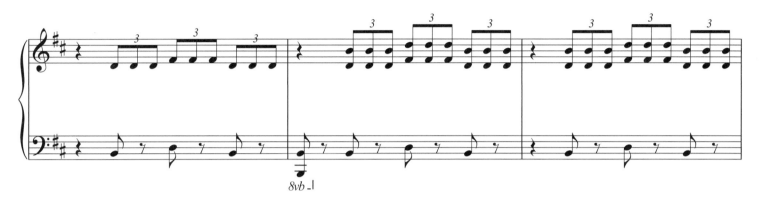

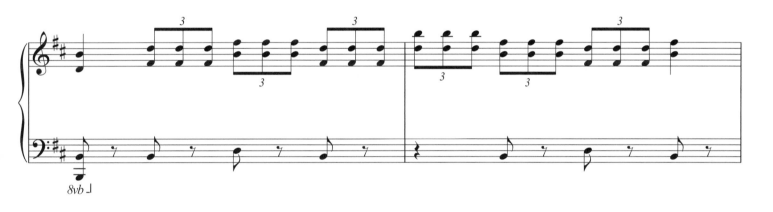

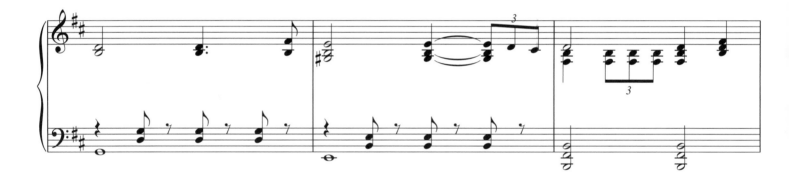

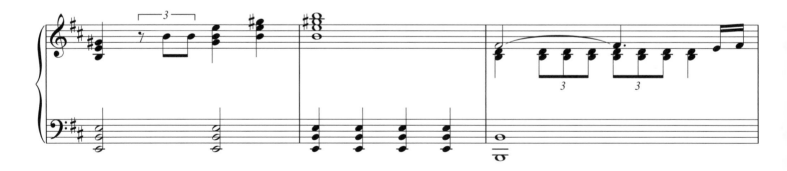

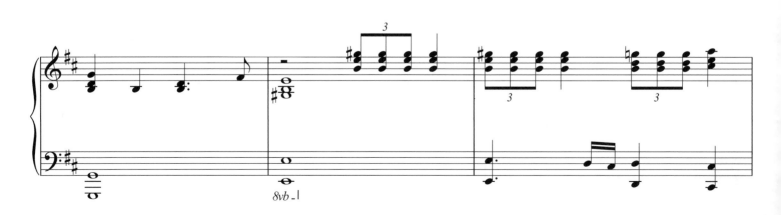

8vb

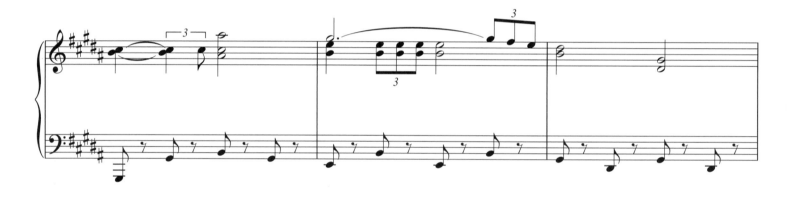

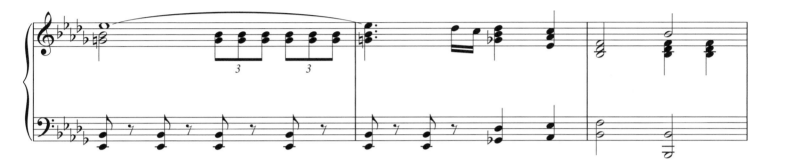

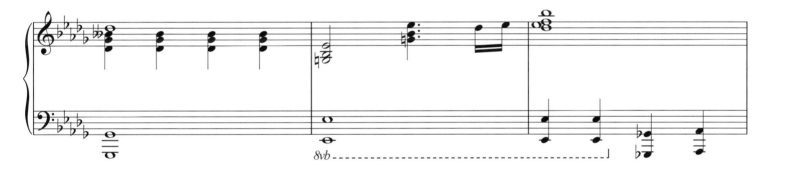

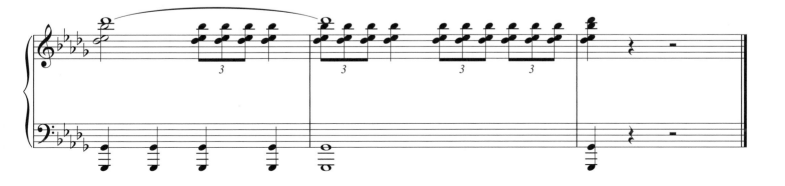

SEE YOU AGAIN
from FURIOUS 7

Words and Music by CAMERON THOMAZ,
CHARLIE PUTH, JUSTIN FRANKS
and ANDREW CEDAR

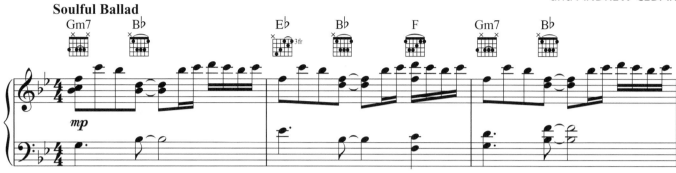

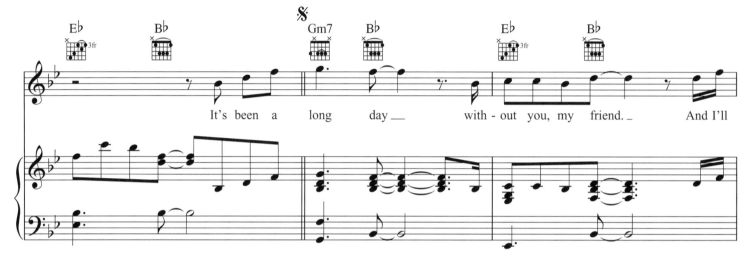

And ev-'ry road you take will al - ways _____ lead you

home, home. _____ It's been a long day ___ with-

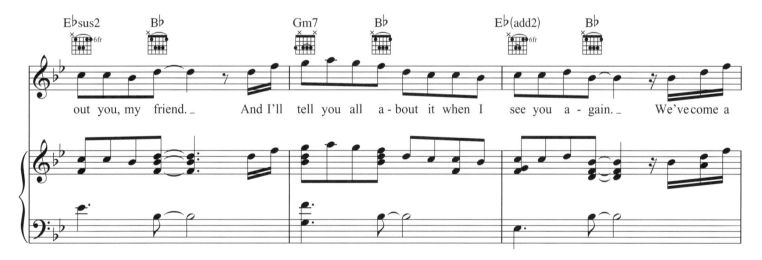

out you, my friend. _ And I'll tell you all a - bout it when I see you a - gain. _ We've come a

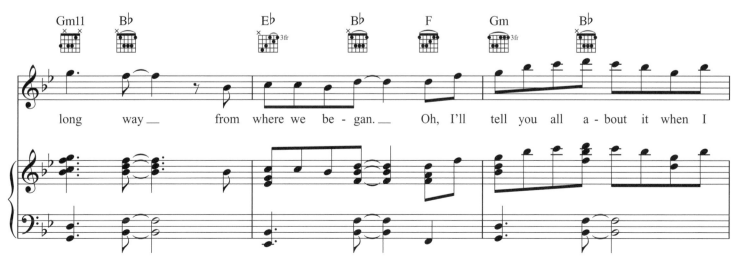

long way ___ from where we be - gan. ___ Oh, I'll tell you all a - bout it when I

118

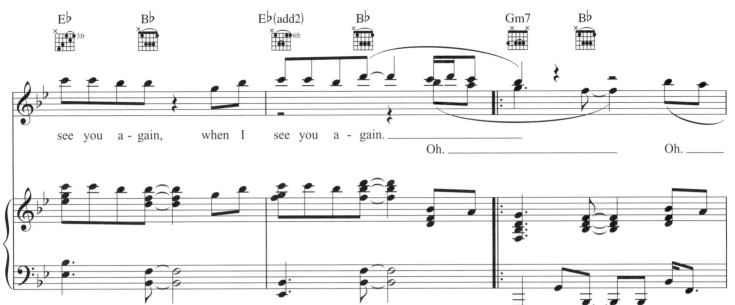

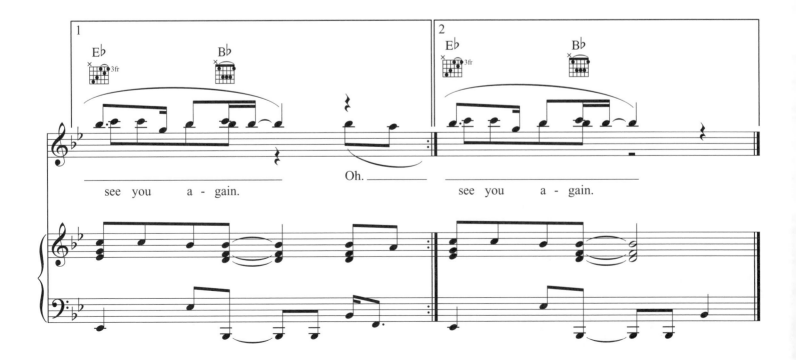

SOPHIE'S FUTURE
from THE BFG

By JOHN WILLIAMS

Moderately slow, expressively

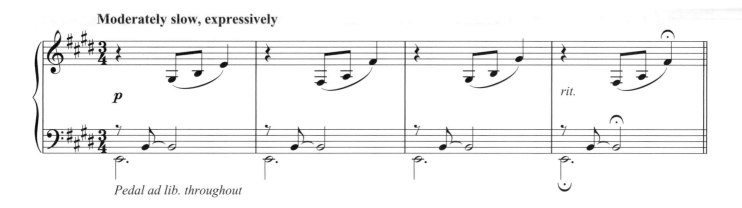

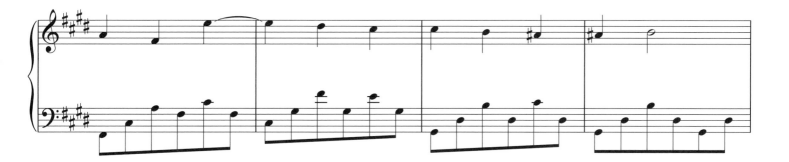

Moderately fast

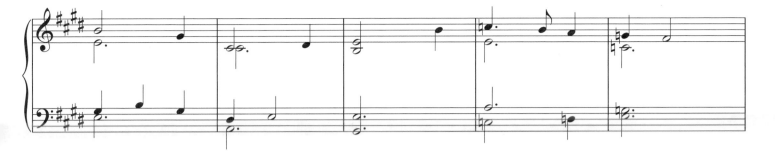

Broadly

SLEDGEHAMMER
from STAR TREK BEYOND

Words and Music by SIA FURLER,
JESSE SHATKIN and ROBIN FENTY

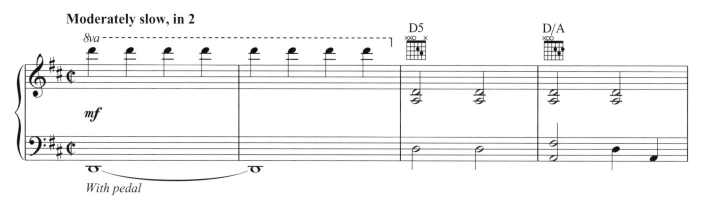

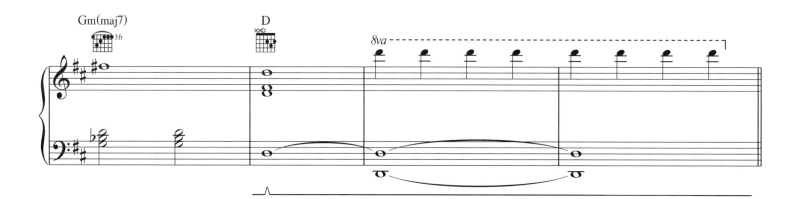

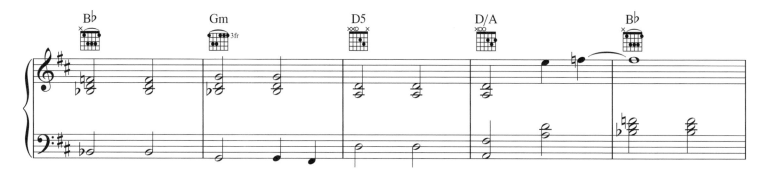

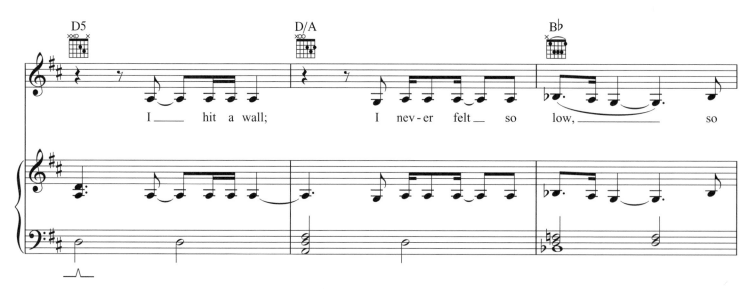

I ___ hit a wall; I nev-er felt ___ so low, _____ so

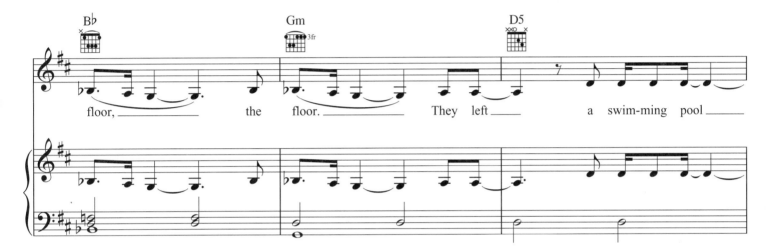

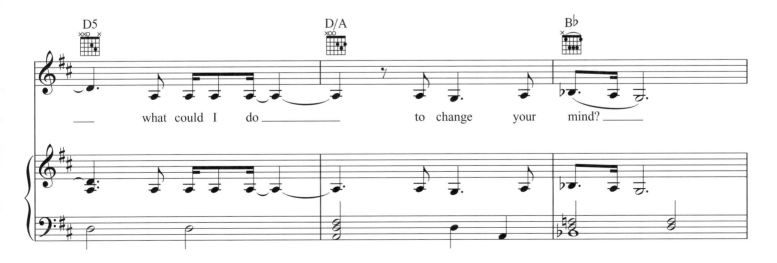

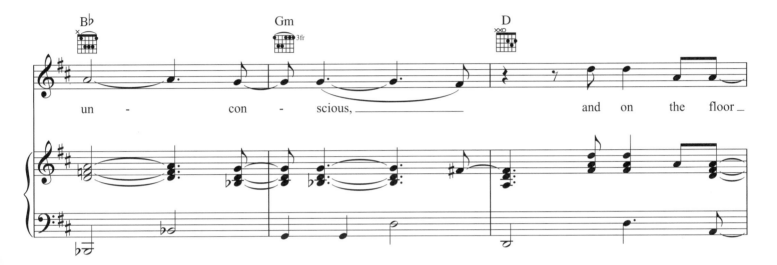

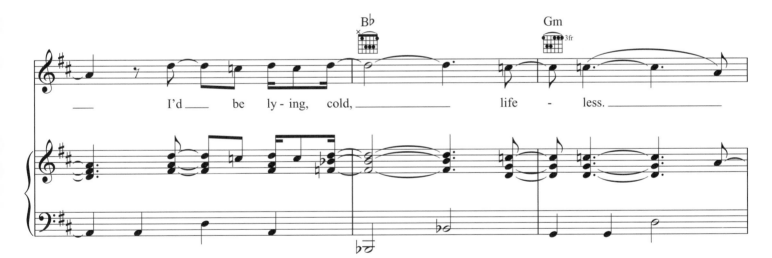

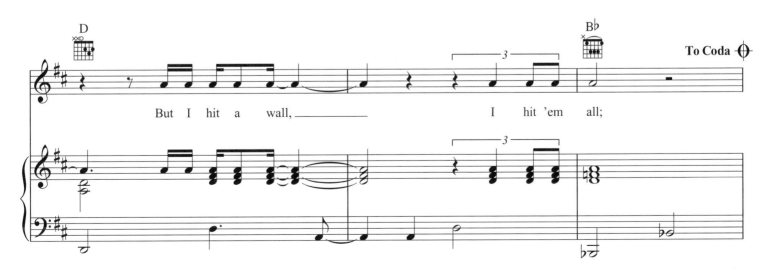

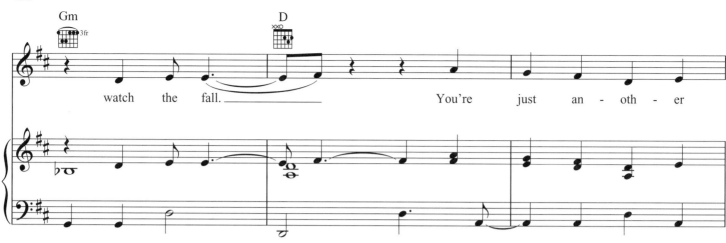

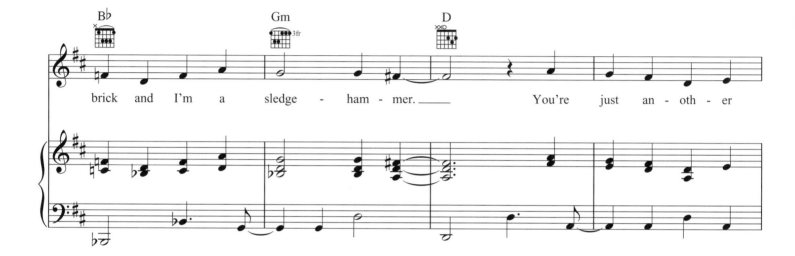

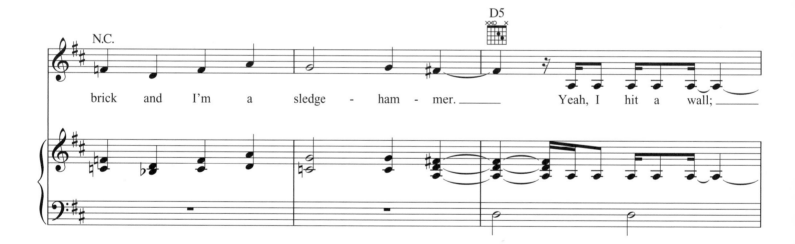

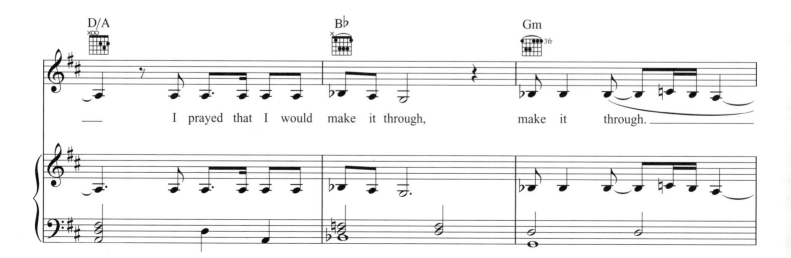

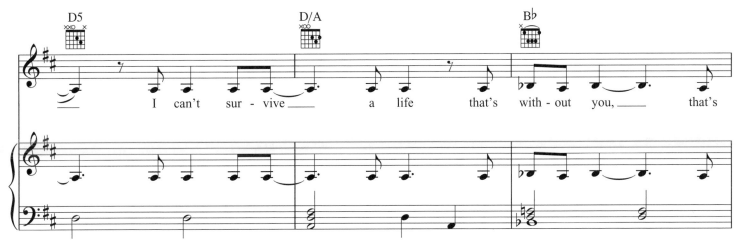

I can't sur - vive _____ a life that's with - out you, _____ that's

with - out you, yeah. _____ And I will rise _____ up from the

ash - es now, the ash - es now. _____ Oh, the spar - row flies _

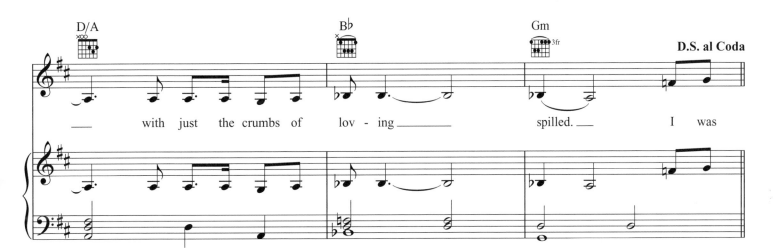

_ with just the crumbs of lov - ing _____ spilled. _ I was

D.S. al Coda

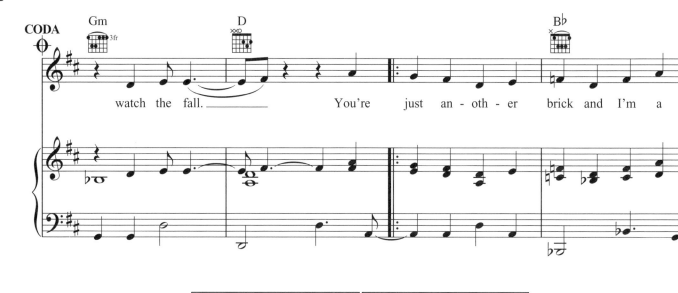

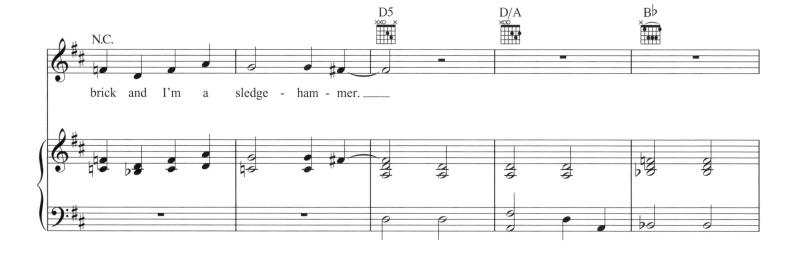

UNSTEADY
from ME BEFORE YOU

Words and Music by ALEXANDER JUNIOR GRANT,
ADAM LEVIN, CASEY HARRIS,
NOAH FELDSHUH and SAM HARRIS

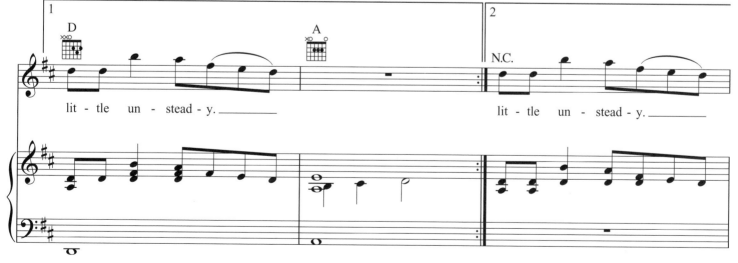

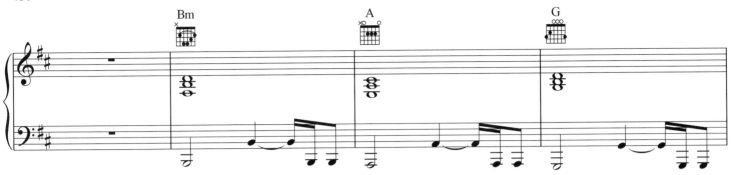

Ma - ma, come here,
Moth - er, I know

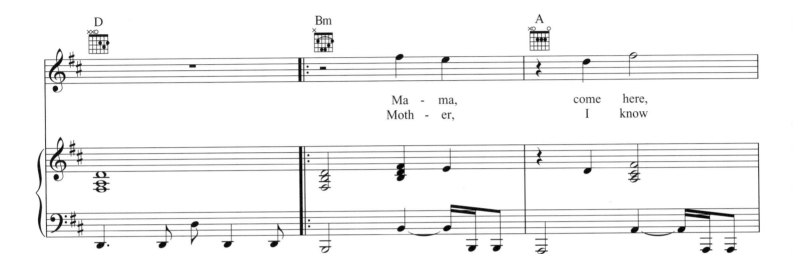

ap - proach, ap - pear. Dad - dy,
that you're tired of be - ing a - lone. _____ Dad, I

I'm a - lone 'cause this house don't feel like home. _____
know you're try - ing to fight _ when you feel like fly - ing. _____

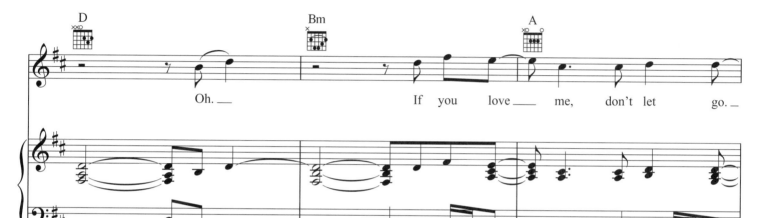

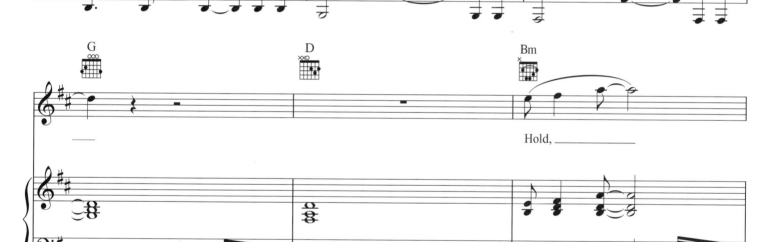

WARM KITTY
featured on the CBS Television Show THE BIG BANG THEORY

Adapted from an English Folk Tune

Warm kit-ty, soft kit-ty, lit-tle ball of fur. Sleep-y kit-ty, hap-py kit-ty, purr, purr, purr. Warm kit-ty, soft kit-ty, lit-tle ball of fur. Sleep-y kit-ty, hap-py kit-ty, purr, purr, purr.

WELCOME TO JURASSIC WORLD

from JURASSIC WORLD

By JOHN WILLIAMS

Slowly, freely

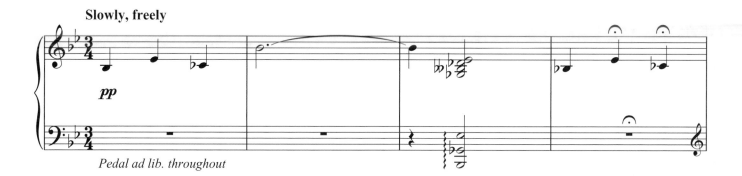

pp

Pedal ad lib. throughout

Slightly faster, expressively

Moderately, steadily

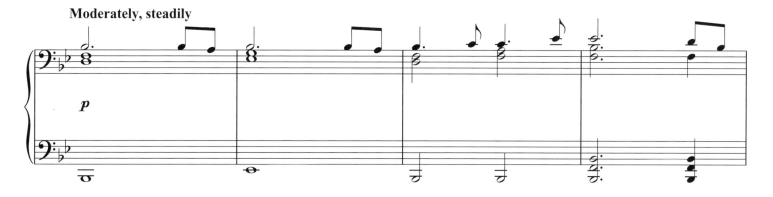

p

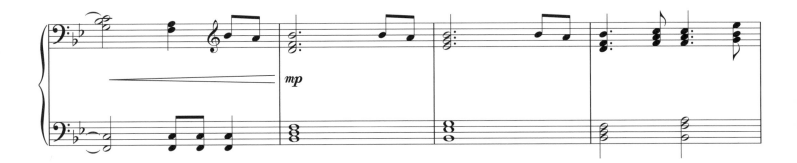

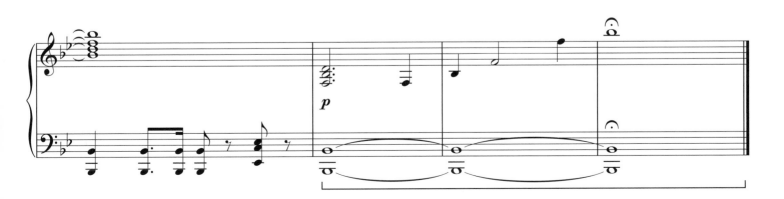

WISH THAT YOU WERE HERE

from MISS PEREGRINE'S HOME FOR PECULIAR CHILDREN

Words and Music by FLORENCE WELCH,
EMILE HAYNIE and ANDREW WYATT

Moderate Alt-Rock

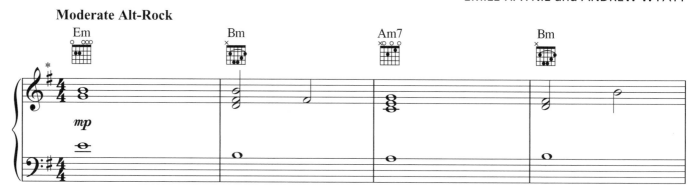

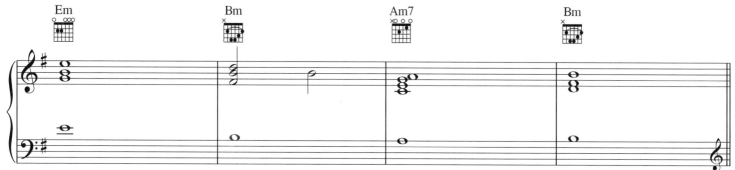

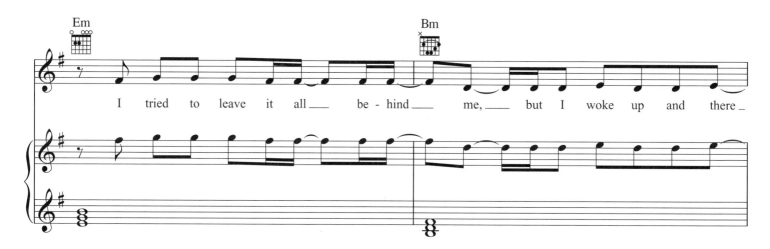

I tried to leave it all ___ be-hind ___ me, ___ but I woke up and there ___

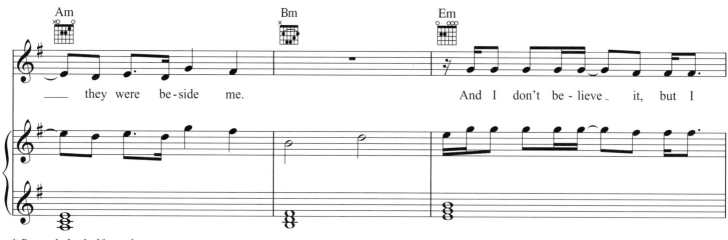

___ they were be-side me. And I don't be-lieve ___ it, but I

* Recorded a half step lower.

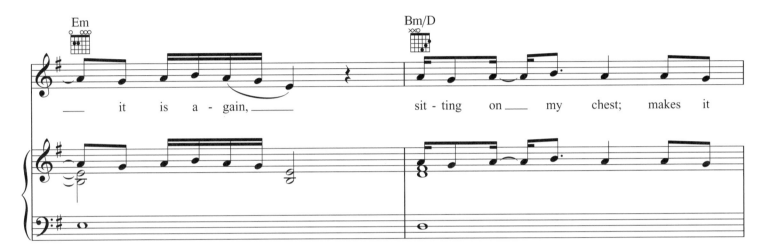

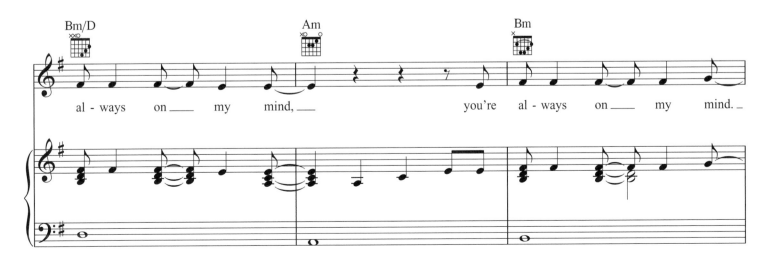

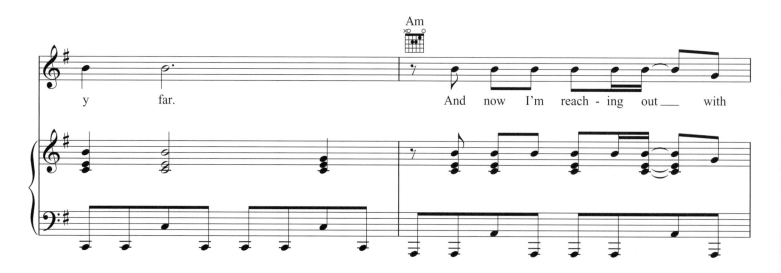

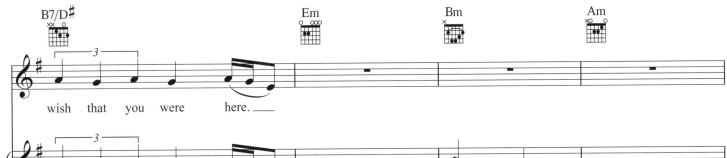

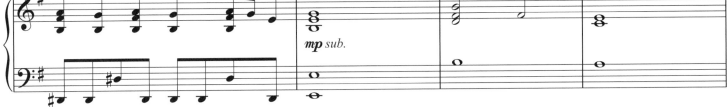

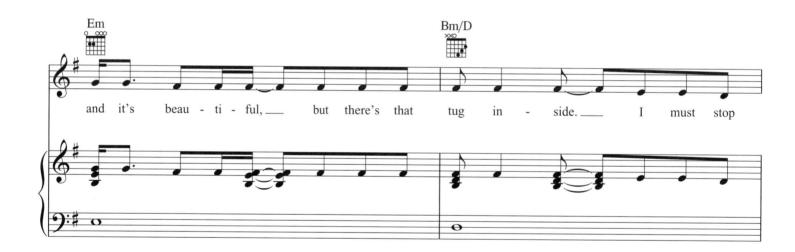

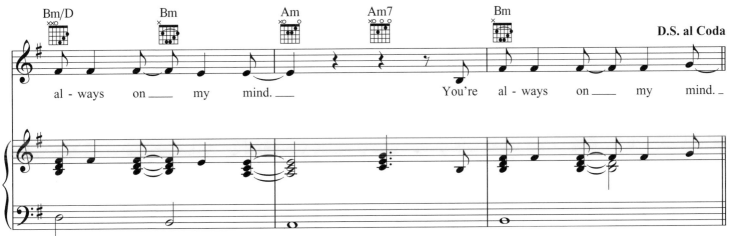

al - ways on __ my mind. __ You're al - ways on __ my mind. _

D.S. al Coda

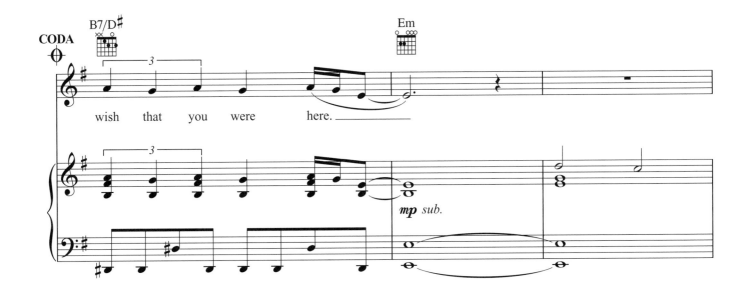

CODA

wish that you were here. ____

mp sub.

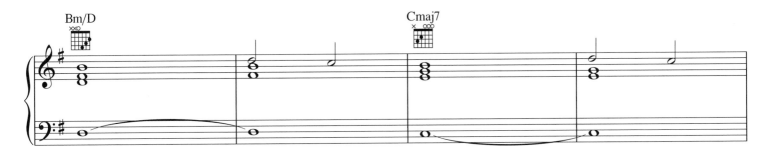

We all need some - thing

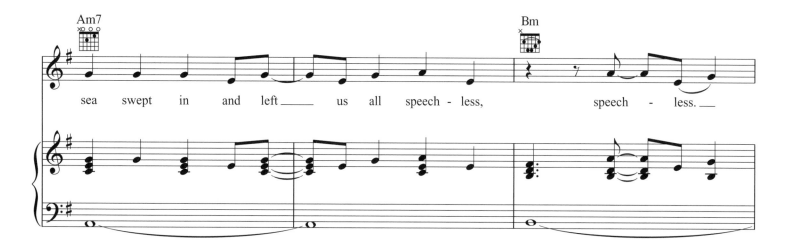

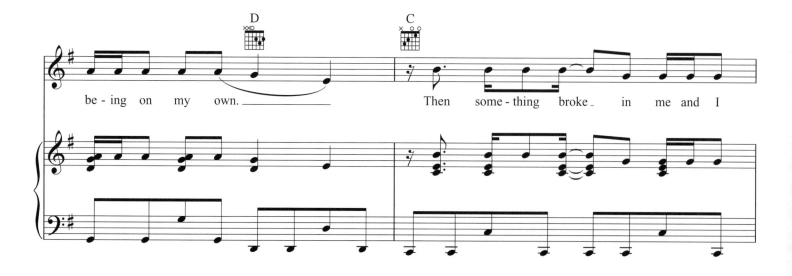

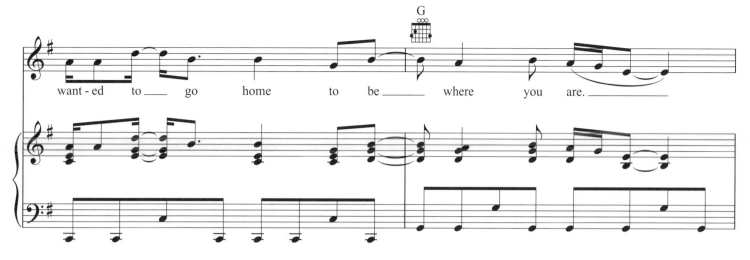

want-ed to ___ go home to be ___ where you are. ___

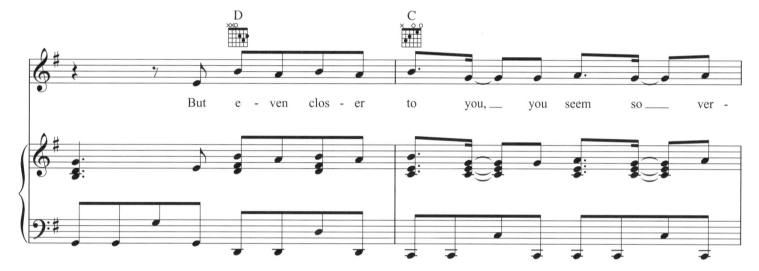

But e - ven clos - er to you, __ you seem so ___ ver -

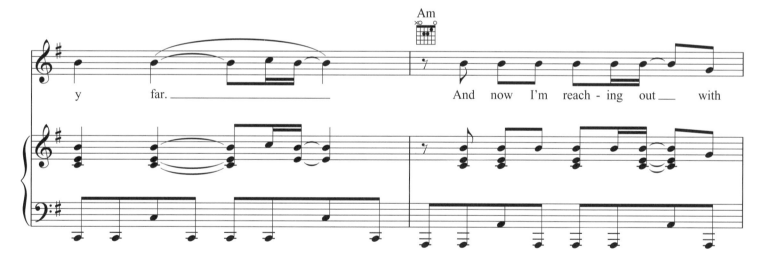

y far. ___ And now I'm reach - ing out __ with

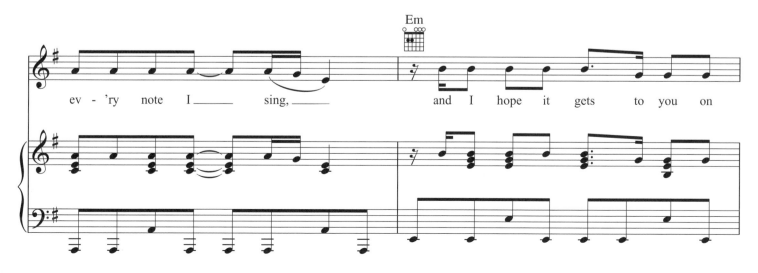

ev - 'ry note I ____ sing, ____ and I hope it gets to you on

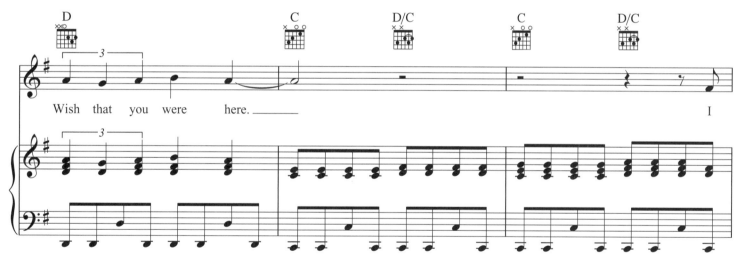

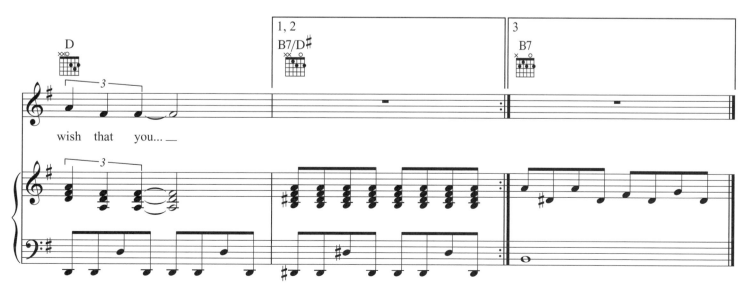

WRITING'S ON THE WALL
from the film SPECTRE

Words and Music by SAM SMITH
and JAMES NAPIER

you, I'm feel - ing some - thing that makes me want to stay. _

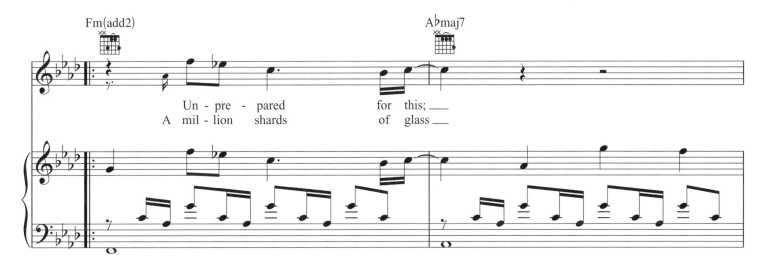

Un - pre - pared for this; ___
A mil - lion shards of glass ___

I nev - er shoot to miss. ___ But I
that haunt me from my past. ___ As the

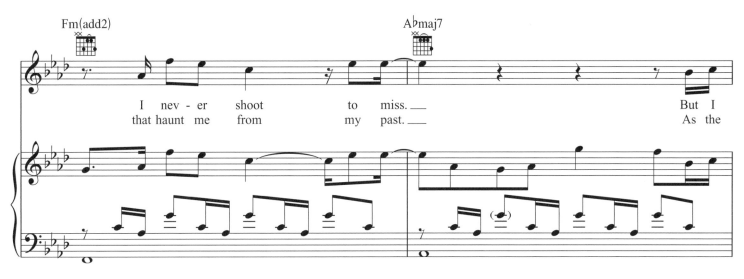

feel like a storm is com-ing if I'm gon-na make it through the day. _ And there's
stars be-gin _ to gath-er, and the light be-gins to fade, _ when all

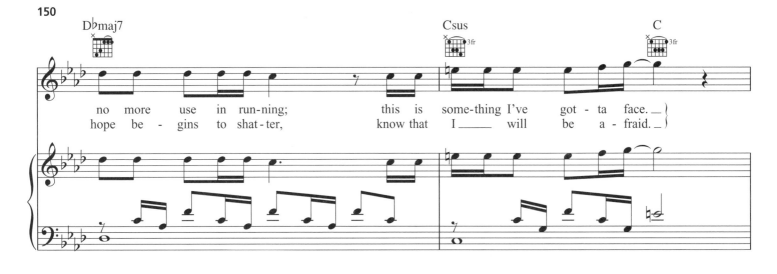

no more use in run-ning; this is some-thing I've got-ta face. __
hope be-gins to shat-ter, know that I ____ will be a-fraid. __

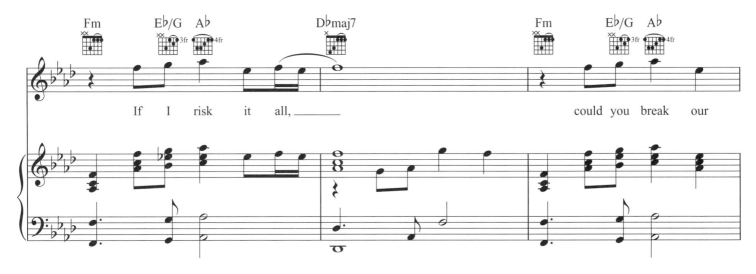

If I risk it all, _____ could you break our

fall? How do I ____ live? How do I breathe? When you're not

here, I'm suf-fo-cat - ing. I wan-na feel __ love run through my blood. Tell me, is

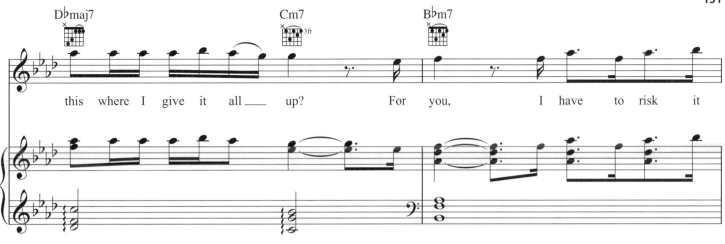

this where I give it all ___ up? For you, I have to risk it

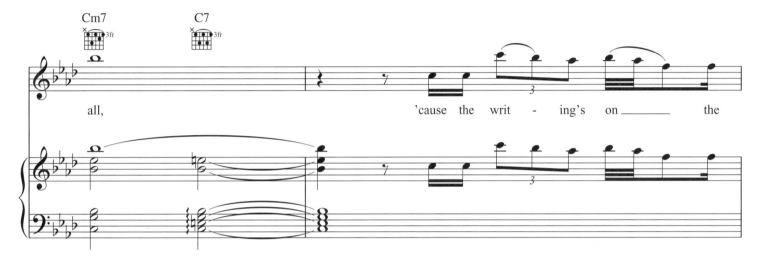

all, 'cause the writ - ing's on _____ the

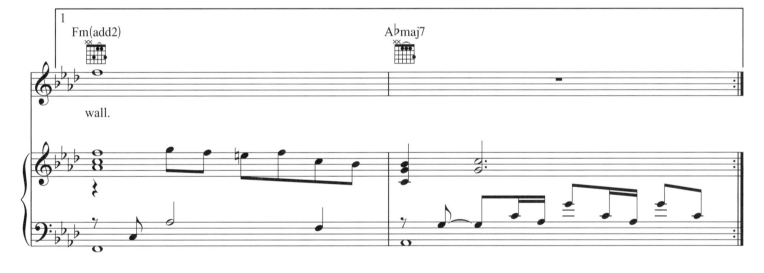

wall.

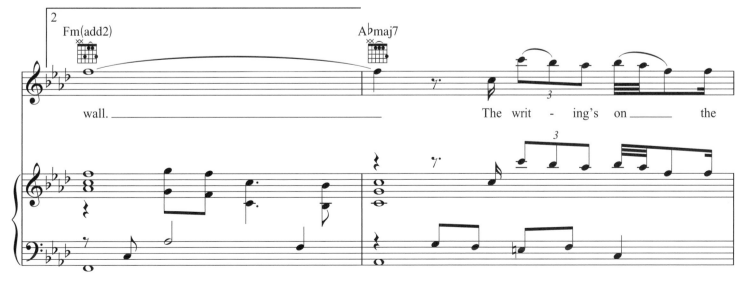

wall. _____ The writ - ing's on _____ the

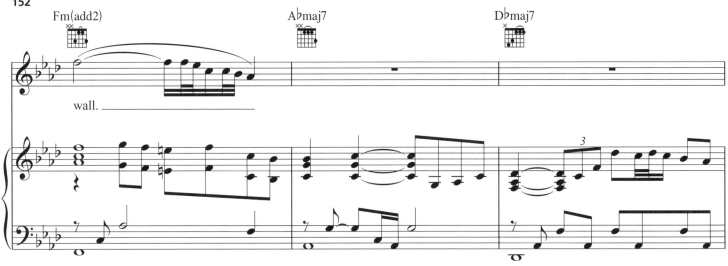

wall. _____

How do I ___

live? How do I breathe? When you're not here, I'm suf-fo-cat-ing. I wan-na feel ___

love run through my blood. Tell me, is this where I give it all ___ up? How do I ___

live? How do I breathe? When you're not here, I'm suf-fo-cat - ing. I wan-na feel __

love run through my blood. Tell me, is this where I give it all __ up? For

you, I have to risk it all,

Freely

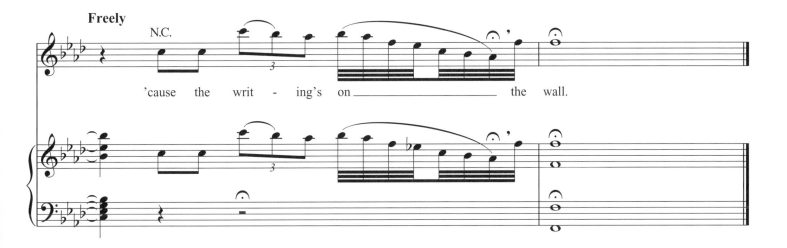

'cause the writ-ing's on __ the wall.

YOU'VE GOT TIME
featured in ORANGE IS THE NEW BLACK

Words and Music by
REGINA SPEKTOR

Driving beat

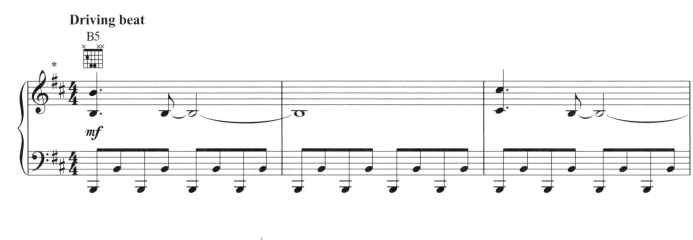

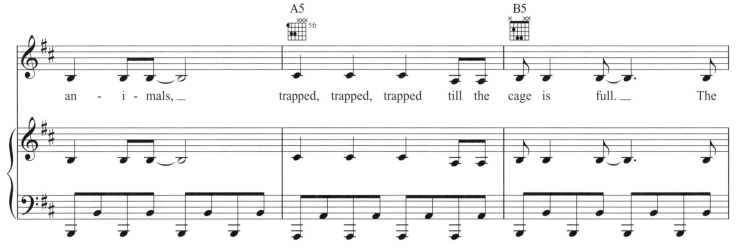

The an - i - mals, ___ the an - i - mals, ___ trapped, trapped, trapped till the cage is full. ___ The

* Recorded a half step lower.

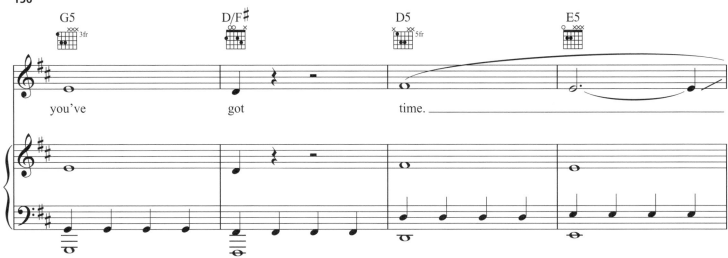

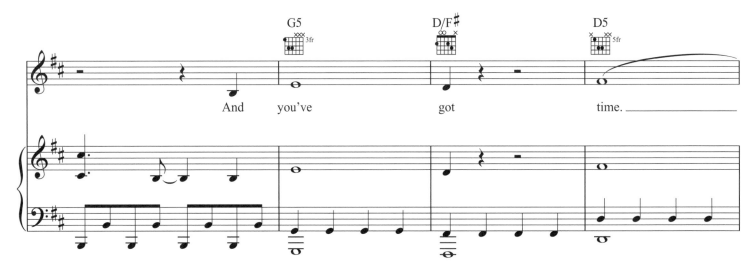

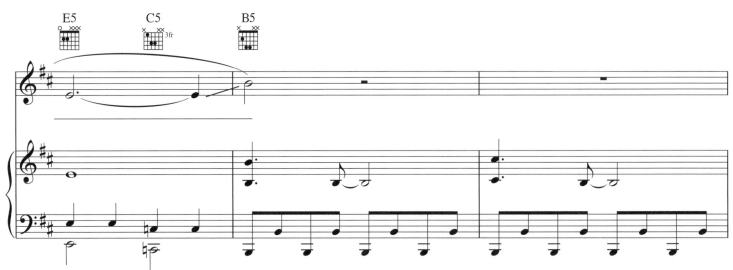

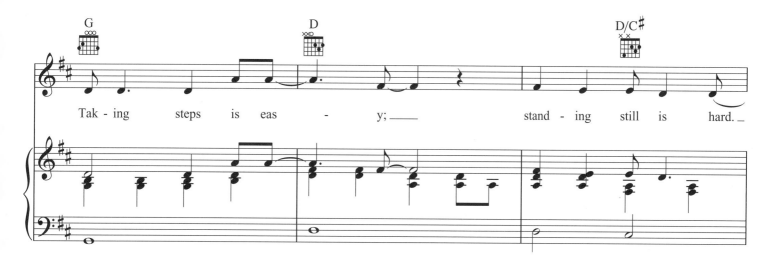

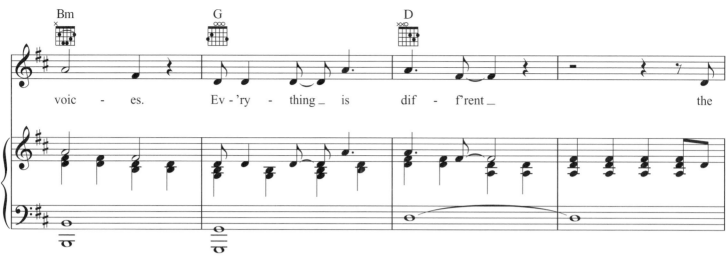

voic - es. Ev -'ry - thing_ is dif - f'rent_ the

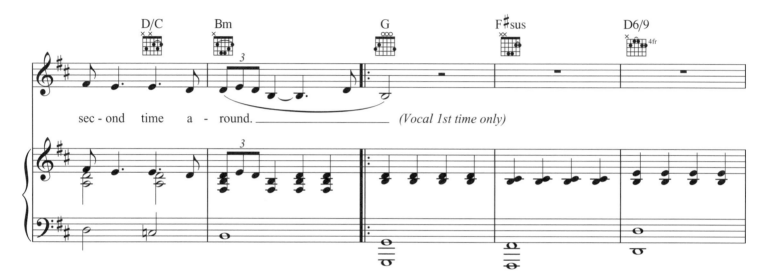

sec - ond time a - round. _____ *(Vocal 1st time only)*

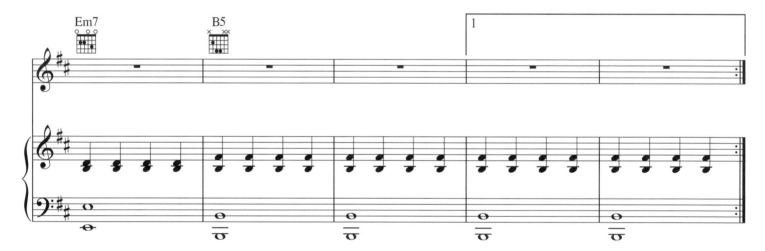

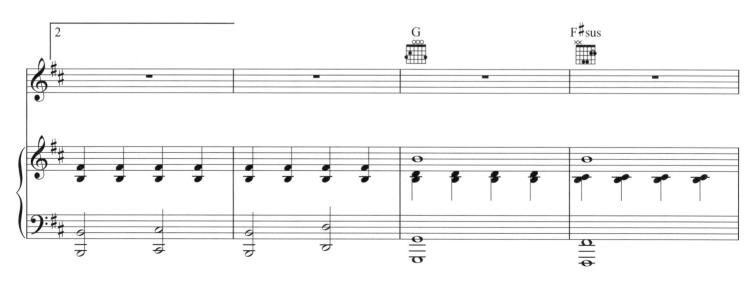

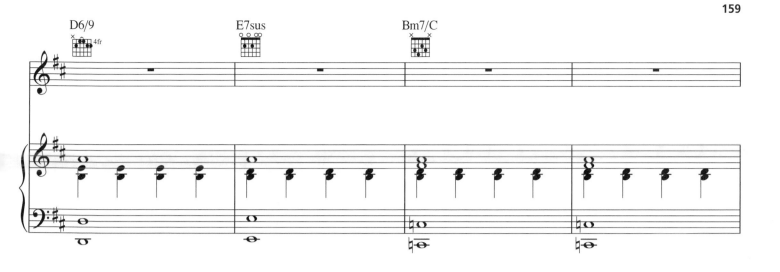

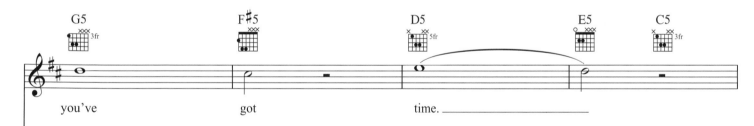

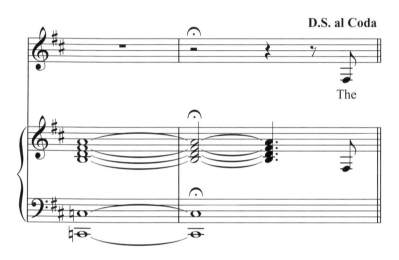

THE BEST EVER

COLLECTION
ARRANGED FOR PIANO, VOICE AND GUITAR

100 of the Most Beautiful Piano Solos Ever
100 songs
00102787 ....$27.50

150 of the Most Beautiful Songs Ever
150 ballads
00360735 ....$27.00

More of the Best Acoustic Rock Songs Ever
69 tunes
00311738 ....$19.95

Best Acoustic Rock Songs Ever
65 acoustic hits
00310984 ....$19.95

Best Big Band Songs Ever
68 big band hits
00359129 ....$17.99

Best Blues Songs Ever
73 blues tunes
00312874 ....$19.99

Best Broadway Songs Ever
83 songs
00309155 ....$24.99

More of the Best Broadway Songs Ever
82 songs
00311501 ....$22.95

Best Children's Songs Ever
101 songs
00159272 ....$19.99

Best Christmas Songs Ever
69 holiday favorites
00359130 ....$24.99

Best Classic Rock Songs Ever
64 hits
00310800 ....$22.99

Best Classical Music Ever
86 classical favorites
00310674 (Piano Solo) $19.95

The Best Country Rock Songs Ever
52 hits
00118881 ....$19.99

Best Country Songs Ever
78 classic country hits
00359135 ....$19.99

Best Disco Songs Ever
50 songs
00312565 ....$19.99

Best Dixieland Songs Ever
90 songs
00312326 ....$19.99

Best Early Rock 'n' Roll Songs Ever
74 songs
00310816 ....$19.95

Best Easy Listening Songs Ever
75 mellow favorites
00359193 ....$19.99

Best Folk/Pop Songs Ever
66 hits
00138299 ....$19.99

Best Gospel Songs Ever
80 gospel songs
00310503 ....$19.99

Best Hymns Ever
118 hymns
00310774 ....$18.99

Best Jazz Piano Solos Ever
80 songs
00312079 ....$19.99

Best Jazz Standards Ever
77 jazz hits
00311641 ....$19.95

More of the Best Jazz Standards Ever
74 beloved jazz hits
00311023 ....$19.95

Best Latin Songs Ever
67 songs
00310355 ....$19.99

HAL•LEONARD®
Visit us online
for complete songlists at
www.halleonard.com

Prices, contents and availability subject to change without
notice. Not all products available outside the U.S.A.

Best Love Songs Ever
62 favorite love songs
00359198 ....$19.99

Best Movie Songs Ever
71 songs
00310063 ....$19.99

Best Movie Soundtrack Songs Ever
70 songs
00146161 ....$16.99

Best Pop/Rock Songs Ever
50 classics
00138279 ....$19.99

Best Praise & Worship Songs Ever
80 all-time favorites
00311057 ....$22.99

More of the Best Praise & Worship Songs Ever
76 songs
00311800 ....$24.99

Best R&B Songs Ever
66 songs
00310184 ....$19.95

Best Rock Songs Ever
63 songs
00490424 ....$18.95

Best Showtunes Ever
71 songs
00118782 ....$19.99

Best Songs Ever
72 must-own classics
00359224 ....$24.99

Best Soul Songs Ever
70 hits
00311427 ....$19.95

Best Standards Ever, Vol. 1 (A-L)
72 beautiful ballads
00359231 ....$17.95

Best Standards Ever, Vol. 2 (M-Z)
73 songs
00359232 ....$17.99

Best Torch Songs Ever
70 sad and sultry favorites
00311027 ....$19.95

Best Wedding Songs Ever
70 songs
00311096 ....$19.95

0916